Tears of

Khwaja Hasan Nizami was born into a Sufi family who were descendants of Hazrat Nizamuddin Auliya and belonged to the Sufi order Chishti-Nizamiya. He was born in 1878 or 1879, twenty years after the 1857 Uprising then known as the *ghadar*. A curious mind steeped in spiritual knowledge, he became interested in the stories of the survivors of Emperor Bahadur Shah Zafar's family, and recorded their experiences in his book titled *Begumat ke Aansoo*.

Rana Safvi is a renowned writer, scholar and translator. She is a passionate believer in India's unique civilizational legacy and pluralistic culture which she documents through her writings, podcasts and videos. She has published eight books so far on the culture, history and monuments of India. These are *Tales from the Quran and Hadith,* The Delhi Trilogy which includes *Where Stones Speak, The Forgotten Cities of Delhi* and *Shahjahanabad: The Living City of Old Delhi*. She has translated both the editions of Sir Syed Ahmad Khan's seminal work on Delhi, *Asar-us-Sanadid* and *Dastan-e-Ghadar*, and four accounts of nineteenth and twentieth-century Delhi from Urdu to English as *City of My Heart* and *A Saint, A Folk Tale and Other Stories: Lesser-Known Monuments of India.*

Also by the translator

City of My Heart: Accounts of Love, Loss and Betrayal in Nineteenth-Century Delhi

Tears of the Begums
Stories of Survivors of the Uprising of 1857

Khwaja Hasan Nizami

Originally published in Urdu as *Begumat ke Aansoo*

Translated by Rana Safvi

First published in 2022 by Hachette India
(Registered name: Hachette Book Publishing India Pvt. Ltd)
An Hachette UK company
www.hachetteindia.com

1

ISBN 978-93-93701-14-5

Hachette Book Publishing India Pvt. Ltd
4th/5th Floors, Corporate Centre,
Plot No. 94, Sector 44, Gurugram 122003, India

Typeset in Arno Pro 11/13.2
by InoSoft Systems, Noida

Printed and bound in India
by Manipal Technologies Limited, Manipal

MIX
Paper from
responsible sources
FSC® C043100

Dedicated to the memory of Khwaja Hasan Nizami
for documenting the tales of the survivors of the
Siege of Delhi in 1857

Table of Contents

	A Note from the Translator	ix
1.	A Picture of the *Ghadar*	3
2.	Bahadur Shah, the Dervish	5
3.	The Princes Get Dragged through the Market	12
4.	The Obstacles Faced by the Orphan Prince	18
5.	The Accursed Princess	24
6.	A Fast Amidst Starvation	29
7.	The Beggar Prince	37
8.	A Family of Royal Descent	41
9.	Bahadur Shah's Daughter	44
10.	The Orphan Prince's Miserable Eid	52
11.	The Grasscutter Saint	59
12.	The Prince Who Drove a Cart	71
13.	The Mendicant's Gift	80

14.	A Destitute Princess Talks to the Vicereine's Photograph	86
15.	The Real Story of the Destitute Princess	91
16.	A Canopy of Dust: The Story of Gul Bano	94
17.	The Misunderstandings That Led to the *Ghadar*	100
18.	The Prince Becomes a Sweeper	109
19.	The Prophet's Descendant: Zakia Bayabani	115
20.	Two Princes in the Jailhouse	132
21.	The Green Clad Woman's War	140
22.	The Grief-stricken Princess	148
23.	The Misfortunes of Nargis Nazar	157
24.	The Kafni	166
25.	Mirza Mughal's Daughter, Lala Rukh	176
26.	The Woman Who Gave Birth During the *Ghadar*	183
27.	The Last Cup of Wine	191
28.	When I Was a Prince	195
29.	The Chef Prince	204
Acknowledgements		211

A Note from the Translator

The Mughal Empire was established by Babur (r. 1526–30) who defeated Ibrahim Lodi, the Sultan of Delhi (r. 1517–26) on the plains of Panipat in 1526. Barring the 15 years that saw Emperor Humayun, Babur's son, defeated by Sher Shah Suri and living in exile till he reclaimed the kingdom, the Mughal dynasty ruled at a stretch till 1857.

The Uprising of 1857, also called the First War of Indian Independence, was a watershed moment in Indian history. In 1857, the last Mughal emperor Bahadur Shah II (r. 1837–57) popularly known as Bahadur Shah 'Zafar', the nom de plume under which he composed poetry, was deposed and exiled to Rangoon by the British East India Company, spelling the end of the Mughal Empire. A year later the East India Company was liquidated, and power was transferred to the British Crown by the Government of India Act 1858.

Though much has been written about the Uprising by both British and Indian authors, and it has been the subject of many novels, the fate of the Mughal survivors and its aftermath remained unknown to the public. There were around 3,000 royals living inside the Red Fort at the time of the Uprising. These included the Emperor and his immediate family, and the descendants of the previous emperors known as *salatin*. The Red Fort and the Salimgarh Fort that adjoined it were densely populated. Immediately after the fall of Delhi, the British secured the walled city of Shahjahanabad and the Red Fort. Harsh and punitive punishments were meted out to the Mughal 'loyalists' and the royal family. In fact, knowing the importance of the Mughal Emperor and the royal family among citizens of the empire, it was only after dealing with them that the British ensured they took action against other 'rebel' centres.

The houses and mansions of the princes and *salatin*s were demolished once the two forts were captured by British forces on 20 September 1857.

Khwaja Hasan Nizami wrote 12 books on the events that unfolded in 1857, all based on eyewitness accounts of survivors. Of these, the most popular collection of stories was *Begumat ke Aansoo* which was first published in 1922. It had gone into thirteen reprints by 1946 and was also published in Hindi, Gujarati, Kannada, Bangla and Marathi. However, a complete English translation of the collection has not been attempted so far. Khwaja Hasan Nizami was born in 1879, when many of these survivors were living in and around Delhi. He met them personally and collected their stories. *Begumat ke Aansoo* is an important document of the events and its catastrophic after-effects on the survivors, the rough and ready and often cruel punishments meted out to the Mughal family often based on false evidence.

The Uprising of 1857 resulted in the wiping out of not only the Mughal Empire but a way of life. The cultural catastrophe has not been fully documented till date. There are references in books such as Ahmed Ali's *Twilight in Delhi* or Mirza Ghalib's *Dastanbuy* and many Urdu accounts of the nineteenth and twentieth century, but much is left unsaid.

In that respect, these tragic stories, based according to Khwaja Hasan Nizami on true facts and his personal research and hard work, are an important testimony to the time.

There are contradictions in some places, but it is important to bear in mind that some of the interviewees were old and had experienced immense trauma. It is natural that there are a few mistakes in their recall, but that does not take away from their basis in truth. Wherever I have found any contradictions, I have mentioned them in references. In some stories the Khwaja has taken the help of a fictionalized narrative as a vehicle to tell the stories he heard, but they remain rooted in fact.

One must also bear in mind that the Khwaja was living at a time when the British were ruling India; that he was able to collect and publish these stories at all is noteworthy. As per a note in the twelfth edition, the book was banned during the First World War by the British government but Sir Malcolm Hailey, who served as Chief Commissioner of Delhi from 1912–18 and later as governor of the United Provinces, allowed its publication. Khwaja Hasan Nizami refers to his lifting the ban when he was the Governor so it must have been sometime between 1928–34.

A descendant of Hazrat Nizamuddin Auliya, Khwaja's birth name was Syed Ali Hasan Nizami, but at some point he dropped the first name and started signing as Hasan Nizami. He was given the title Khwaja by the famous philosopher-poet Allama Iqbal for his knowledge and spiritual attainments.

I have referred to three Urdu editions of *Begumat ke Aansoo* for this translation, as successive editions kept adding new stories and making additions to existing stories. I accessed the twelfth edition which was published by Ibn-e Arabi Karkun Halqa-e Mashaekh, Delhi in 1934 and the thirteenth edition published by Aalimi Press, Delhi in 1944 from the Rekhta Foundation e-books section. The third book is a compilation of all the 12 books written on the *ghadar* of 1857 by Khwaja Hasan Nizami and published in 2008 by the Khwaja Hasan Sani Nizami as *1857, Shamsul Ulema Khwaja Hasan Nizami ki Barah Qadeem Yaadgar Kitabein*. I have followed the table of contents of this new edition after consulting the Pakistani original *Majmua Khawaja Hasan Nizami 1857* published in 2007 by Sang-e-Meel Publications on which the Indian edition was based. The only liberty I have taken is to move the chapter 'A Picture of the *Ghadar*' to the beginning so that the reader can get a clearer idea of the stories that follow, and in a few instances I have changed the titles to give the reader a better idea of the content.

I am extremely grateful to Syed Mohammed Nizami, grandson of Khwaja Hasan Nizami and nephew and executor of the estate of Khwaja Hasan Sani Nizami (son of Khwaja Hasan Nizami) for giving me permission to translate *Begumat ke Aansoo*.

Rana Safvi

Shahr Ashob
Lament for a City

Zewar almas kaa tha jin se naa pahna jaata
Bhaari jhumar bhi kabhi sir pe naa rakhha jaata

Gauze kaa jin se dupatta naa sambhala jaata
Laakh hikmat se orhaate to naa orha jaata

Sar pe bojh liye chaar taraf phirte hain
Do qadam chalte hain mushkil se tau phir girte hain

The delicate ones who couldn't carry the weight of precious gems
For whom heavy jewellery was a burden too heavy

Those who found dupattas of gauze a heavy burden
Despite contrivance who couldn't keep their veil in place

Those frail ladies, are made to carry heavy loads, alas
They can barely walk a few steps before they fall down

— Mufti Sadruddin Azurda on the fall of Delhi in 1857

1

༞ Pictuɾe of the Ghadaɾ[1]

Allah! How many poignant and emotional scenes are hidden in time! The same Delhi that saw the blood of innocents flowing down its streets now takes on new hues. Babur's sword had once killed Ibrahim Lodi and the former ruler's family stood helplessly before the new Emperor. Now, Babur's descendants have lost their power and are vulnerable in these terrible times.

When I entered the Dilli Durbar, my glance fell on a picture[2] that showed the last scion of the Timurid empire, Abu Zafar Bahadur Shah, being arrested by Major Hodson at Humayun's tomb. Bahadur Shah stood wearing his cloak, holding a staff in his hand. His face reflected his sorrow and powerlessness, and his wrinkles revealed his advanced age. Major Hodson, in his red uniform, held the emperor's hand in his, not in salutation, but in supreme victory.

---

1. This note comes in the middle of a few stories in the new edition named, *1857, Shamsul Ulema Khwaja Hasan Nizami ki Barah Qadeem Yaadgar Kitabein* (1857: The Twelve Old [and] Memorable Books of Shamsul Ulema Khwaja Hasan Nizami] published in 2008 by Khwaja Hasan Nizami's heir, Khwaja Hasan Nizami Sani. I have kept it at the beginning to give a context to the stories that follow.
2. An illustration of the emperor's arrest appeared in the book *The Indian empire: its history, topography, government, finance, commerce and staple products* by R. Montgomery Martin published in 1860 by the London Printing and Publishing Company Limited. It depicts the emperor surrendering to Major Hodson.

Two of Hodson's soldiers stood behind the emperor. A loyal Mughal soldier was leaping forward to strike Hodson, but before he could do anything one of Hodson's soldiers had already shot him dead.

Alas! How can one still crave for power?

As I was leaving, my glance fell on a page from the *Diwan-e Hafiz*[3] whose first verse read:

Aakhir nigah ba su-e makin
Ai Daulat khas o hasrat aam

Finally, turn your glance at me,
O wealth of the rich and yearning of the poor
—Hafiz

I came out reliving the capture of the Emperor and reciting these lines.

---

3. Though Khwaja Hasan Nizami credits the verse to Hafiz, it was actually written by Sheikh Sadi.

2

Bahadur Shah, the Dervish

The last emperor of Delhi had the temperament of a dervish.[4] Myriad tales of his ascetism are popular in Delhi and around Hindustan. Even today, there are many alive who saw this dervish emperor and heard his spiritual verses.

Bahadur Shah was a very devout man. Since work related to governance was in the hands of the British, he had all the time in the world for the remembrance of God and to write spiritual verses. Even when the durbar was held and the courtiers had gathered, he would discuss not matters of state but of spirituality. He would discourse on mysticism and gnosis.

The custom was that when the courtiers gathered in the Diwan-e Aam or Diwan-e Khas, Huzur Zill-e Subhani would prepare to leave the mahal. As soon as the *badshah* was ready to leave, the female *naqib*, the herald, would call out, *'Hoshiyar, adab qaiyda, nigahdar.'* Lal Purdah was the *deorhi* attached to the Khas Mahal.[5] From here

---

4. Religious mendicant
5. Lal Purdah was the name given to the area in the courtyard nearest to Diwan-e Khas, leading to the emperor's private apartments called Khas Mahal, screened by red broadcloth cloth. No other male member except the emperor and princes of the royal blood could go beyond the Lal Purdah. Eunuchs called *khwajasaras* and female attendants made announcements from this point onwards.

the male *naqib* would hear her call and echo it in the Diwan-e Aam or Khas, wherever the durbar was being held. On hearing this announcement, the courtiers would stand in their places as per protocol.

It was a unique sight to see the nobles and ministers standing there with bent necks, eyes lowered, hands clasped in front of them. Not one of them dared to lift their eyes or move their body unnecessarily. They would be in a state of awe and all movement in the durbar would be stilled.

The moment Huzur Zill-e Ilahi emerged out of the *deorhi* on his moving throne, the royal sedan-chair, the *naqib* would call out, 'The Zill-e Ilahi has appeared. Present your *mujra*, salutations, with respect.' On hearing this one noble would come forward respectfully and stand on the station of salutation and would bend double and present three *kornish*[6] to the emperor. While the noble was presenting his *kornish*, the *chobdar*, or the usher, would call out his credentials and rank and draw the Emperor's attention to the *kornish*. All the nobles and courtiers present would come forward and present their salutations in a similar fashion.

When all the salutations had been presented, Huzur Sultan would proclaim, 'Today I have said a ghazal,' and would then read the first verse. On hearing the verse, one noble would leave his place in the durbar and come to the station of salutation and say humbly, 'Subhan Allah. The words of an emperor! An emperor's words!' He would then return to his place.

With every verse one of the nobles present would fulfil the duty of a listener by praising the words. From the beginning, Bahadur Shah's verses were mystical, filled with a pain that would serve as an admonition for mankind. So much so that behind his cheerful exterior a kind of helpless despair could be felt by all listeners.

Bahadur Shah would take on spiritual disciples and all those who took the oath of allegiance were given a stipend of five rupees a month. Thus, many would take the oath with him. Many say that

---

6. *Kornish* is the salutation in which one bends double and raises one's palm to the forehead by bringing it up in an arc from the ground.

Bahadur Shah himself had taken an oath of allegiance with Hazrat Maulana Fakhr,[7] but Bahadur Shah was very young when Hazrat Maulana sahib was alive and it seems unimaginable that he would have taken an oath of allegiance at that age. Yes, he was placed in the venerable Maulana sahib's lap as a child. After the respected Maulana sahib's death, Bahadur Shah benefitted from the guidance of his son Hazrat Miyan Qutbuddin and he took an oath of allegiance with him. The emperor shared a special bond with Miyan Qutbuddin's son, Miyan Nasiruddin, popularly known as Miyan Kale sahib: so much so that he wed his daughter to Miyan Kale sahib.

The emperor was himself an enlightened dervish and was always eager to meet all dervishes and mendicants but he had a special affinity and devotion for Sultan al-Mashaikh Khwaja Nizamuddin Auliya Mehboob-e Ilahi. He would often visit the saint's shrine. He was on very good terms with my maternal grandfather Hazrat Shah Ghulam Hasan Chishti, towards whom he showed much respect. My grandfather would go often to the Qila and attend the special assemblies arranged by Bahadur Shah. My respected mother would often tell me stories about the Emperor which she had heard from her father. Even though as a child, I had no idea of the grandeur and greatness of the Emperor, I was instinctively drawn to these stories and would reflect on the impermanence of this world.

Bahadur Shah was an enlightened mystic who had imbibed spiritual knowledge of the unseen. He had divined the events of the *ghadar* much before the event took place through his spiritual powers but was content to place his trust in the will of God. Thus, when Hazrat Shah Allah Baksh Chishti Sulaimani Tonsvi came to Delhi for the first time, Bahadur Shah invited him to the Qila. After the meal was over, the emperor excused everyone and when he was left alone with Hazrat sahib he asked him about the hidden [divinely ordained] reason for the tottering condition of his empire.

Hazrat Tonsvi replied, 'I think your ancestors have committed some grave mistakes of which the gravest is that they have put up a

---

7. Muhammad Fakhr-ud-Din sahib was a prominent saint of the eighteenth-century. He died in 1784–85.

barrier between the lover and the beloved.' Or, to put it in words, Emperor Mohammed Shah had been buried between the shrines of Hazrat Mehboob-e Ilahi and Hazrat Amir Khusrau.[8] The extreme love between Hazrat Mehboob-e Ilahi and Hazrat Amir Khusrau dictated that no one should come between their shrines. For Hazrat Mehboob-e Ilahi had said that had it not been forbidden by the Sharia they would have been buried in the same grave. In such a case it was completely wrong for Mohammed Shah to be buried in between and that was the cause of the destruction being faced by the empire.

My grandfather used to say that these words had a profound effect on Bahadur Shah who believed them with all his heart.

Thus, he knew through manifest and latent means that the decline of the empire was imminent and he would repeatedly express this thought in his private conversations.

The *Urs* Procession

Whenever Bahadur Shah went for the *urs* of Hazrat Mehboob-e Ilahi, there was a grand spectacle. The final ceremony which marked the end of the *urs*, would be put on hold till he graced the occasion. As soon as his cavalcade entered, there would be a huge fuss that the Emperor had arrived. On seeing the Emperor enter the dargah, the hordes would make way for his procession and walk in a single file from the gateway to the shrine. The Emperor would pay his respects at the blessed shrine, and then join the assembly. The *khatm*[9] ceremony would then start, followed by the qawwali.

---

8. The shrine complex of Hazrat Nizamuddin Auliya contains two shrines of the saint, and his favourite disciple, Hazrat Amir Khusrau. The Mughal emperor Mohammad Shah willed his grave to be in front of the saint's shrine, thus coming in between the master and disciple. According to oral history records, the Emperor forced the hand of the hereditary caretakers to give him that piece of land for his grave.

9. A ceremony held after death or during the *urs* celebration at which prayers and Qur'anic verses are recited by way of benediction.

The Emperor would leave after listening to one ghazal. The moment he got up to leave, the teeming crowds would split once again to make a way for the royal procession.

The Era Between Royalty and Impecunity

If Bahadur Shah had not been involved in the *ghadar*, he would have lived the life of a dervish with comfort and ease. But he got caught in the trap set by the rebel forces and spent the last days of his life in great misery.

My mother heard from her father, Hazrat Khwaja Shah Ghulam Hasan, that the day the emperor left the Qila of Delhi, he went straight to the dargah of Mehboob-e Ilahi. He was in a state of despondency and despair. Only a few eunuchs and the porters carrying his sedan chair were with him. His face was lined with worry and his clothes were covered in dust. His white beard was matted with dirt.

On hearing that the emperor had come to the dargah, my grandfather presented himself before His Majesty. He found him leaning near the head of the shrine. A faint smile appeared on his face when he spotted my grandfather. He sat in front of the emperor and asked him about his well-being.

The emperor replied with great simplicity, 'I had said these accursed rebels were headstrong and trusting them was a mistake. They were bound to go down and take me with them. This is what has transpired. Now they have run away. I am a mendicant, but I am a descendant of the Timurid race, which has the instinct and courage to go down fighting. Even though my ancestors went through tough times, they never gave up hope. But my end has already been revealed to me. I am undoubtedly the last Timurid to sit on the throne of Hind. The lamp of the Mughal dynasty is about to be snuffed out: it shall last only for a few more hours. Why then should I indulge in unnecessary bloodshed? That's why I left the Qila myself. This country now belongs to God and He can bestow it on whomever He pleases. For hundreds of years, my ancestors ruled Hindustan through force and fear. Now it is time for others to rule. We will become the ruled and they shall be the rulers. There is no reason to mourn, for we too removed someone from the throne and destroyed their dynasty to establish ours.'

On completing his monologue, the Badshah handed over a box to my grandfather, entrusting it in his care. 'When Amir Timur conquered Constantinople, he acquired this box from the treasure of Sultan Yaldram Bayazid. It has five strands of hair from the blessed beard of our beloved Prophet. It has been passed down in our family as a special blessing. Now there is no place for me in this wide world, and I don't know where I can take it. I am placing the box in your care as you are the worthiest person I know. These strands of hair have provided much solace to my weary heart over the years. Today, on the most calamitous day of my life, I must part with them.'

My grandfather took the box from the Badshah, and carefully placed it in the treasury of the dargah. The box remains with us even today, and on every twelfth day of Rabi al-Awwal visitors to the dargah might catch a glimpse of it.[10]

[Having discharged his duty towards his precious charge] the Badshah told my *nana* sahib, 'I have not had time to eat the last three meals. If there is some food in the house, please bring it for me.'

'We are also standing at the edge of death and no one has had any time, or peace, to cook. But I will bring whatever I can for you. In fact, why don't you grace my humble abode with your blessed presence? As long as my children and I are alive, no one can touch you. We will die before anyone can harm you,' *nana* sahib said.

'I am grateful for your kindness, but I will not jeopardize the lives of my *pir*'s children to defend this old body. I have paid my respects to Mehboob-e-Ilahi,[11] and I have entrusted you with my beloved treasure. Now, if I can eat a few morsels, I will go to Humayun's tomb. Destiny will fulfil what fate holds in store for me.'

Nana sahib rushed home and asked if there was something to eat. He was told that only *besani* roti,[12] a chutney made of vinegar,

---

10. This custom continues till date.
11. Hazrat Nizamuddin Auliya
12. Flatbread made from gram-flour

and some relish were available. He took the food on a covered tray and presented it to the *badshah*, who ate it and thanked God for His mercy.

Thereafter, he left for Humayun's tomb, where he was arrested and later exiled to Rangoon, where he continued his spiritual pursuits. Until he breathed his last, he was a forbearing and pious dervish.

This tale should serve as a warning to all humans. After hearing it they should give up pride and ego. Only then can man become human.

3

The Princes Get Dragged through the Market

Delhi, the heart of India, its capital, was flourishing. When the flame of the Mughals began to flicker, and the Empire was teetering on the precipice of destruction, the first noticeable change was in the lifestyle of its people. Both, rulers and subjects, were destroyed.

I

A year before the mutiny, a few princes had gone into the jungle for shikar. They were hunting doves and other birds that were resting on the branches of the trees, shielding themselves from the hot summer sun. A faqir dressed in rags presented his salaam with great respect and said, '*Miyan sahibzado'n*, why are you tormenting these innocent birds? What wrong have they done to you? They too are living beings. They can feel pain just like you but can't express their helplessness. Show them mercy, for they too are citizens of this country and deserving of royal clemency.'

The eldest prince, who was eighteen years old at the time, was embarrassed and kept his slingshot away. The younger one, Mirza Nasir al-Mulk, fumed with anger and said contemptuously, 'Go away, you! A worthless man like you wants to preach to us? Who are you to tell us what to do? Everyone hunts. We are not committing a sin.'

The faqir said with humility, 'Sahib-e Alam, don't get angry. We must only hunt in a manner such that even if one animal is killed, at least a few people can feed from it. What can you achieve by killing these tiny birds? Even if you kill twenty of them, not a single man's belly can be filled.'

This further enraged Mirza Nasir and, aiming his slingshot at the faqir's leg, he shot a stone at his knee. The faqir fell face forward.

'You have broken my leg!'

Without paying any heed, the princes mounted their horses and left for the Qila. The faqir dragged himself to a nearby cemetery and kept repeating, 'How can a dynasty flourish with heirs so merciless? Young Prince, you mercilessly broke my leg. May God break your leg too and force you to drag yourself around, just like me.'

II

A year later, the sound of cannons and gunshots filled Shahjahanabad, and heaps of corpses were lying around everywhere. Delhi was being deserted. A few dishevelled and bewildered Mughal princes were seen riding from the Lal Qila towards Paharganj.[13] They were being chased by 25 British soldiers on horseback, who let loose a volley of gunshots. Very soon, the horses and princes were found writhing in pain on the ground. When the British soldiers approached them, they realized that two princes were dead—but one was still breathing. A soldier pulled him to his feet and found that he was unhurt barring a few scratches he had got from falling off the horse. He was, however, frightened out of his wits due to the strange turn of events.

The soldiers tied his hands to the reins of his horse and sent him off to the camp on the ridge accompanied by two soldiers. Indian soldiers who were supporting the British had gathered there. When the senior officer learnt that the prince was Nasir al-Mulk, the

---

13. Paharganj was just outside the walled city of Shahjahanabad and many families sought shelter there after the fall of the walled city to the British.

grandson of the emperor, he was very pleased and asked that the captive be kept safely.

III

Once the rebel sepoys started fleeing in disarray and the British army entered the city in triumph, Bahadur Shah was arrested from Humayun's tomb and the lamp of the Timurid dynasty was snuffed out. The jungles around Delhi began filling up with Mughal princesses in disarray, their hair and faces dishevelled and uncovered. Fathers were slaughtered in front of their children, while mothers witnessed their sons writhing in the dust in the throes of death.

Mirza Nasir al-Mulk was sitting at the edge of the ridge tied up with ropes when a Pathan soldier came to him and quietly said, 'Run away, I have taken permission from sahib to release you. Go before they catch you again.'

The poor Mirza was at a loss for he had never travelled on foot. However, his survival instincts were strong and, thanking the Pathan, he set off. He walked around aimlessly for a mile, but soon his feet began to blister, his throat was parched, and his tongue swelled up. Unable to bear it anymore, he collapsed under the shade of a tree and looked imploringly towards the sky.

'O Lord, why has this calamity struck us? What should I do? Where can I go?'

He saw a dove hatching eggs in a nest on the tree. Envious of her freedom, the prince said, 'O dove, you are a thousand times better than me. At least you sit without a care in your nest. There is no place for me in this whole wide world.'

The prince spied signs of habitation in a distance and, gritting his teeth, decided to move towards it. The blisters on his feet began to bleed, but he somehow managed to reach his destination. Here, he witnessed a macabre spectacle. Hundreds of villagers surrounded a platform on which a thirteen-year-old girl sat in a state of complete shock. Her ears were bleeding from where her earrings had been wrenched off, and the villagers were laughing at her. As soon as

Mirza and the girl laid eyes on each other, they screamed in shock. The girl was his sister. They embraced each other and wept bitterly. The princess had left the Qila with her mother in a *rath* for Mehrauli to take refuge in Qutub sahib's dargah. Mirza had no idea that she had been caught in the onslaught.

'Malika, how did you end up here?' he asked.

'Aakaa[14] ji, the Gujjars looted us and killed the servants. People from another village forcibly took Ammajan to their village and these people brought me here. They snatched my earrings and kept slapping my face.'

She was crying so uncontrollably by now that she could hardly speak. The Mirza wiped his sister's tears and began to plead with the villagers to let her go.

The Gujjars said with contempt, 'Go away, you are a fine one to talk like this. If we hit you even once, your neck will separate from your body. We have bought her from those villagers. Now you can buy her from us.'

'Chaudhry, I am not in any position except to beg for food from you. Please have mercy on us. Until yesterday we were your rulers and you were our subjects. Please don't torture us. We are going through a hard time. If we come back to power, we will reward you handsomely,' Mirza replied.

The villagers laughed loudly, 'Oho, the Emperor! We will now sell you to the *firangi* and this girl will serve our village. She will sweep it, look after the cattle and clean up after them.' While they were talking, the British forces arrived and surrounded the village. They arrested the Gujjar chief, and the young prince and princess.

IV

Gallows had been erected in the bazaar of Chandni Chowk to hang whoever the British pronounced as guilty. Thousands were hanged every day. Some were shot, and others decapitated with

---

14. Elder brother

swords.

Mirza Nasir al-Mulk and his sister were presented before the *Bade sahib*,[15] who pronounced them innocent and let them go. The two managed to find employment with a trader. The princess looked after his children and Nasir al-Mulk did the chores, including buying provisions for the house. Within a few days, the princess died of cholera which was raging in the city. The Mirza then took up jobs at various houses.

Finally, the British government fixed a monthly pension of five rupees for all Mughal princes, and he no longer needed to seek employment.

Some years later, a *pir* baba, a mystic, who looked like he belonged to the Timurid-Chengezi lineage, could be seen dragging himself around the Chitli Qabr and Kamra Bangash. He couldn't move his legs as they were paralysed, and he had a bag around his neck. He would meekly look at passers-by and ask for help. Those who knew who he was would throw a few coins into his bag. When people asked who he was, they were informed that he was Mirza Nasir al-Mulk, the grandson of Bahadur Shah.

Once a prince, Mirza Nasir wasted away his pension and took heavy loans against it. Now begging was his only means of surviving.

There is a lesson to be learnt from the life of Mirza Nasir. The faqir's curse had come true. I heard this tale from him and some other princes. Whenever I remember it, my heart quakes with fear. The sight of the crippled prince dragging himself in the bazar can fill the hardest of hearts with pity and make them fear divine retribution.

Now the prince is dead.

Will not our proud and arrogant brothers learn from the story of this prince and shed their egos, when the end of egotism is before them?

Most of all I would like to warn the children of the sheikhs who are getting spoilt by the adulation their fathers receive from their disciples and think no one is their equal. If one does not develop one's own character and gain knowledge, and instead depends on

---

15. Person in charge

the glory and power of their ancestors then they are surely paving the way for their own disgrace and downfall. Each *pirzada*, sons of the hereditary caretakers in the shrine, should acquire knowledge or skill that made their ancestor a *pir*. It is shameless to expect offerings from the devout without making oneself worthy of it.

I have seen many *murshidzadas*, sons of saints, who lead a life of luxury from childhood and order their father's disciples around as if they are their subjects or dependants. But in the same way that destiny destroyed monarchy and brought the princes to their knees and forced them to beg in lanes, this new era is bent on destroying spiritual rule too. It should not be that like the princes, the *pirzadas* too should be jolted out of their comfortable existence and forced onto the streets. There is still time. We should all learn our lesson and improve our lives and priorities to face adversity with courage and determination. We should contribute towards making our peaceful environment safer and better.

I say this now and I will continue saying this till my pen and my tongue let me do so.

4

The Obstacles faced by the Orphan Prince

Mah-e Alam was the maternal grandson of Emperor Shah Alam. He was only eleven years old at the time of the *ghadar*. Similar to the other royals, his father Mirza Nauroz Haider received a stipend of hundred rupees from the treasury of Bahadur Shah. However, his mother inherited a large treasure from her father and he didn't care about this paltry sum. He lived sumptuously like the royal princes.

When the *ghadar* began, Mah-e Alam's mother was sick. Her treatment was ongoing, but every day the disease seemed to worsen. So much so that on the same day that Bahadur Shah left the Qila and the agitated residents of the city were running around, she left this world. At a time when everyone was worried about their lives, this death caused great despair. There was no way to procure a shroud or make arrangements for the burial. No woman was available to give the ritual bath to the dead body before the burial. It was customary for the professionals who took care of the shroud, burial and funeral rites to perform this task before royal burials. Because of the widespread suffering due to the *ghadar* no such person was available. Of the two slave girls present in the house, neither knew how to give a ritual bath. Mirza Nauroz Haider was well educated and well versed in religion but he had never had to undertake such work, so he had no idea how to go about it.

The family had spent a few perplexed hours trying to figure out what to do in this distressing situation, when they heard that the British forces had entered the city and were about to come into the Qila. Upon hearing this, the Mirza panicked and quickly put the body on a cot and started washing it. He poured a few urns of water on the body and since there was no way he could get a shroud in a city where all shops were shut, he wrapped his wife in a white bedsheet. He was wondering where to bury her, for he could not take the body outside, when some white and Sikh soldiers entered the house and arrested him and Mah-e Alam. Then they started looting the house, breaking open boxes, ripping apart the cupboard doors and burning the books. A soldier spotted the two slave girls hiding in the bathroom. He dragged the poor wretches out by their hair.

Though these soldiers knew that there had been a death in the house and the dead body was yet to be buried, they continued with their looting without giving it much thought. When they were done looting, they tied everything up in bundles and put them on the heads of the two slave girls, Mirza and his son, herding them out like pack horses.

Mirza cast one last despairing glance at his wife's unshrouded body. It lay there unattended, waiting for burial. But he had no choice but to leave it alone thus.

The slave girls were used to carrying around loads on their heads. Even Mirza Nauroz Haider was a strong man, so he could easily bear the burden. But poor Mah-e Alam was in a sorry state. Apart from the fact that he was carrying a load far heavier than he could at his age, he had a delicate build. The physical pain added to the emotional loss from his mother's death. His eyes were puffed up and swollen from crying the whole night. He was moving in and out of bouts of dizziness. The load on his head coupled with the naked swords behind him and fierce commands pushing him to walk faster made the poor boy stumble. Panting hard he said to his father, 'Abba Hazrat, I am unable to walk, my neck is about to break from this load, I am dizzy and I fear I'll fall down any minute.'

Hearing his beloved and only son's anguished appeal, the distressed father turned to the soldiers and said, 'Sahib, let me carry my son's load. He is sick and might faint.'

The white man following them could not understand what the Mirza said. He punched him hard for stopping and being impertinent. The poor Mirza withstood the blows but took his son's bundle and tucked it under his arms. The white man was angered by this act. He snatched the bundle and put it back on Mah-e Alam's head, punching him hard for disobedience in the process.

Unable to see this cruelty being inflicted on his darling son, the Mirza threw aside his bundle and slapped the white man's cheek hard, following it up with a punch on the nose. Fountains of blood erupted as the nose split.

The Sikh soldiers had parted from the group and only two white soldiers were taking the prisoners to the camp. Seeing his comrade's state, the second soldier hit Mirza with his bayonet but by God's grace he missed his target and the knife barely scraped the side of Mirza's waist. The Timurid prince grabbed this opportunity and punched the soldier's face. As with the first soldier, this punch was so hard that the second soldier's nose was broken too and blood started pouring out. Forgetting their pistols and spears, the two soldiers pounced on Mirza and started pounding him with their fists. The two servants threw their bundles and picking up fistfuls of dust from the ground threw it into the eyes of the white soldiers. This confounded the white soldiers for a few minutes. Taking advantage of their confusion, Mirza snatched their swords. Once he had secured the sword, Mirza gave a strong blow to one of the soldiers, killing him immediately with a deep cut on his chest. Then he beheaded the second soldier. With the two soldiers dead, Mirza turned towards his son only to find that Mah-e Alam had fainted. When the father picked him up, he opened his eyes and putting his arms around Mirza's neck started sobbing.

Mirza was standing still when some ten or twelve soldiers, white and Sikh, approached from behind. Seeing their two comrades lying dead on the ground, they separated the boy from the father and surrounded Mirza to question him. Mirza narrated the entire sequence of events as truthfully as he could. The soldiers were angered beyond measure on finding out how Mirza had killed the two white soldiers and immediately fired six shots from their pistol. Mirza fell to the ground. Leaving behind Mirza Nauroz's corpse, they took Mah-e Alam, the two slave girls and all the loot to their camp.

Once the tumult of the capture of Delhi died down, the two slave girls were given to two Punjabi officers and Mah-e Alam was appointed to serve an English officer. As long as the officer lived in Delhi, Mah-e Alam wasn't troubled too much. He had very little to do since the officer had many servants and cooks to do whatever was required, but after sometime this officer returned to England and handed over Mah-e Alam to another officer in the Meerut cantonment. The second officer had a harsh temperament. He would punch and hit the boy at the littlest of opportunities. Unable to bear the daily beatings, Mah-e Alam decided to run away. He made his way out at night and when the sentry questioned him, he said his English employer had asked him to go to so and so village for some work and return by morning. The excuse worked, and Mah-e Alam ran away into the jungle.

Setting off on an unfamiliar path, scared of being caught, fearful of the unknown, the young boy was in a difficult predicament. By morning he had made it a few miles away from Meerut. He found shelter in a mosque in a village nearby. Mah-e Alam tried to ward off the questions of the maulvi who wanted to know from where he had come and where he was headed. A mendicant who was also staying in the mosque took pity on the young boy with a sweet face and calling him near gave him some leftover food to eat. Finding him to be a sympathetic ear, Mah-e Alam told Shah sahib his story from beginning to end. The boy's heart-rending tale brought tears into Shah sahib's eyes. He embraced the boy and offered words of comfort. 'You don't have to worry anymore. Now you will stay with me for God is the guardian and helper of the distressed,' he said.

Shah sahib clad the boy in a coloured garment and they set off. Initially, Mah-e Alam tired easily and they needed to rest immediately but after a while the boy got used to the speed and could keep pace. In a month they reached Ajmer sharif. Here they met Shah sahib's *pir* who had come from Baghdad. When he heard Mah-e Alam's story, he was also sympathetic and took both of them with him to Bombay. The Shah sahib from Baghdad used to live in Bandra and that is where Mah-e Alam started living too. Here he learnt the Quran, read books on shariah and became well-acquainted with matters regarding Islam.

When he matured, Mah-e Alam asked the Baghdadi Shah sahib if he could take an oath of allegiance with him. Shah sahib replied, '*Miyan*, you are already like my disciple.'

However, Mah-e Alam said, 'Respected Sir, please admit me into the folds of your *silsilah*, your Sufi order, and teach me the path of Sufism.'

Shah sahib's eyes welled with tears. He replied, 'It is not easy to become a Sufi disciple. People consider it to be child's play but it is a tough path. They want to be inculcated as disciples of a Sufi order without understanding the rules, responsibilities and duties involved. The obstacles you have faced till today will pale in front of the tests that you will have to face at every step of this path. Baba! The path of mendicancy is filled with a thousand obstacles.

'These days people want to become disciples so that they can fulfil their desires. Although mendicancy means giving up on all worldly desires once you catch the hem of the *pir*, but if these followers can't rid themselves of desires, they request the *pir* to help them annihilate these worldly desires!

'*Miyan sahibzade*, mendicancy is also a kind of empire. Just as emperors appoint able officers to handle affairs of state, the mendicants also need enlightened and spiritually aware people to help them. The reason Bahadur Shah had to face defeat at the hands of the British was that he did not have able men to help and guide him. How else did he lose to a handful of British officers when the whole country was sympathizing with him? The British won because of their abilities and superior knowledge of administration, while the Emperor lost. The life of a dervish is the same. Man's base desires and Satan keep tempting him day and night to give up his faith and go towards the path of wealth and prosperity. The mendicants defeat their enemies through their inner wisdom and powers to perform miracles but once they lose their spiritual powers, Satan can easily lure them away from their faith. These days the mendicants have also forgotten the rules of their order. That is why their disciples are also floundering. You need to first understand everything the path entails to become a disciple before you come to me with this request.'[16]

---

16. In the twelfth edition of the Urdu book (1934), this conversation between Mah-e Alam and Shah sahib about becoming his disciple is missing. It ends on the line, 'Shah sahib got him married off to a sweet-tempered girl and Mah-e Alam settled down in Bandra.' This last line was missing in the book that I largely relied on for the present translation: *1857, Shamsul Ulema Khwaja Hasan Nizami ki Barah Qadeem Yaadgar Kitabein* which is a 2008 compilation, and instead of this line, there is an important comment on the Sufi path.

5

The Accursed Princess

'Even though the *ghadar* took place 50 years ago, I remember it as clearly as if it were yesterday.

'My name is Sultana Bano. My father, Mirza Quwaish Bahadur[17] was a beloved and able son of Hazrat Bahadur Shah. I was sixteen years old then, two years younger than my brother Mirza Yavar Shah, and six years older than my sister Naaz Bano, who died. We sisters were very fond of our brother, Yavar Shah, and our affections were reciprocated fully. *Aakaa bhai*[18] had a whole range of tutors who taught him every subject and instructed him in various arts. He had expert calligraphers, Arabic and Persian scholars as well as ace archers teaching him. We sisters learnt embroidery, stitching and other household arts from *mughlanis*[19].

'The children whom Huzur-e wala[20] was fond of used to eat breakfast with him every morning. Zill-e Subhani[21] was fond of me, and I was always called to join the breakfast table. We did not

---

17. The British appointed Mirza Quwaish Bahadur as the crown prince in 1856, over the claims of Zeenat Mahal's son Mirza Jawan Bakht.
18. *Aakaa* is a term of respect meaning elder brother.
19. Female attendants, seamstresses in the Mughal harem
20. His Exalted Presence
21. The Shadow of God on Earth

observe purdah then, and do not do so now either. Strangers would come and go from the women's palace without any problem. But I was shy, so I kept my head covered and preferred not to be in front of strange men. However, I had to obey the orders of Huzur, even though various male cousins would attend the breakfast. The saving grace was that they kept their gazes lowered because they were in the presence of the emperor. No one could look up or speak out of turn.

'As per the custom, Huzur-e Mo'alla[22] would offer a morsel from a special dish to a few of his children. The child, whether young or adolescent, boy or girl, would get up from their seats, walk up to him, and present three salaams with bows. One day, Huzur gave me a portion of a special Irani dish that had been made that day. He said, "Sultana, you only peck at your food. It's good to be respectful, but you should not go to the extent that you get up hungry from the *dastarkhwan.*"

'I presented three salutations to him that day, but only I know how I was quaking and tripping over my feet while I went up to him and walked back.

'Alas! Where did those happy days go? What happened to that era? We would roam about in our palaces without a care in the world. Zill-e Subhani's benevolent shadow was over our heads and we were addressed as Malika-e Alam. Such are the ups and downs of life.

'I clearly remember the day when Huzur-e Mo'alla was arrested at Humayun's tomb. A white man[23] shot my *chachajaan* Mirza Abu

---

22. His Exalted Presence

23. A description of this event is given in Khwaja Hasan Nizami's book 'Dilli ki Jan Kuni' (The Agony of Delhi). Events during the Mutiny relating to the Royal Family, The Nobility, and the Hindu and Muslim Residents of Delhi, translated by A Sattar Kapadia. I quote from that (please note that in Kapadia's translation, Major Hodson's name has been spelt as Major Hudson):

'Munshi Zakaullah has stated that, "On the second day of the capture of the Badshah, Munshi Rajab Ali and Mirza Ilahi Bux reported that Mirza Mughal and Mirza Khazr Sultan the two sons of the Badshah and his nephew Mirza Abu Bakar were also in the Tomb of Humayun and these were the very men who were responsible for the murder of the British women and children in the Fort. Major Hudson was furious at this news and after taking permission from General Wilson

Bakr Bahadur. Mirza Sohrab ran towards the white man with a naked sword, but he was shot down by his comrade. He fell with an 'aah' on top of chachajaan's[24] corpse and joined him in heaven. I stood there, mute and still as a statue, watching it all. A eunuch came to me and said, "Begum, why are you standing here? Your father is calling you."

'I followed him in a state of stupor.

'Bare-headed and anxious, my father, Mirza Quwaish Bahadur, was seated on a horse near the river gates. Abbajan's hair were covered in dust and straw. He started crying when he saw me and said, "Farewell, Sultana, I too am leaving. The light of my life, my young son, whose face I wanted to see behind a sehra of pearls and flowers on his wedding day, was killed in front of my eyes by a Sikh soldier."

'I screamed loudly, "O my brother Yawar."

'He dismounted and pacified Naaz Bano and me. He said to me, "Daughter, the British are now looking for me. I don't know how long I can remain out of their clutches, or how long I have before my life is snuffed out. You are, by the grace of God, young and sensible. Pacify your younger sister, place your trust in God, and be

---

he departed on his mission to murder the Princes. Mr MacDonald also accompanied Major Hudson. Taking 100 instead of 50 riders with him, he went to the Tomb and at that time he was accompanied by the spies Munshi Rajab Ali and Mirza Ilahi Bux.

All three Princes were inside the Tomb, but in spite of his large force, Major Hudson was again reluctant to enter the Tomb as the Princes were surrounded by a group of their fierce supporters.

Just like their father, the Princes refused to surrender until they were given guarantees of safe conduct and a promise that they would not be harmed. Major Hudson replied that he had no authority to give any such guarantees to them as he was under the command of General Wilson.

They said their farewells to their sympathizers and came out of the Tomb.

When the Princes came in front of Hudson, he glared at them but kept quiet. He ordered them to get into four wheeled carriages; they were then surrounded by Hudson's men and started moving towards Delhi.

When they were one mile outside Delhi, Hudson ordered them out of the carriages and remove their clothes. The Princes looked at each other but at that point they were not aware that their lives were in danger. They had been given reassurance that Hudson had no powers to take their lives." They were shot by Hudson and their bodies stripped and hung on the Lal Darwaza near Firoz Shah Kotla. This earned the Darwaza the name of Khooni Darwaza'.

24. Father's younger brother

patient. I don't know what will happen to either of us. I don't want to leave you both alone, but one day or the other, you will both be orphaned. Naaz Bano is a child, look after her and live a righteous life." Then he spoke to Naaz Bano, "You are no longer a princess, so don't throw tantrums or make demands. Just give thanks to Allah and eat whatever you get. If someone is eating, don't look at them, or the people will say princesses are greedy."

'He put the eunuch in charge of us and said, "Take them to where the other members of our family have gone." With that, he gave us a last embrace and spurred his horse into the jungle. That was the last we saw of him; we have no clue what happened to him. [25]

'The eunuch was an old servant of our family. He set off with us. Naaz Bano walked a little, but she had never walked such a distance in her pampered and protected life so far. Soon, her legs gave way, and she began to cry. I had never walked much myself either, but I managed somehow and, pulling Bano along, stumbled through the streets where we once rode elephants in state processions. When a thorn pricked Naaz Bano's foot, she fell down. I tried to remove the thorn. The accursed eunuch watched us but made no effort to help. Instead, he started pushing us to hurry up.

---

25. Mirza Quwaish escaped to Udaipur in the aftermath of the 'Ghadar' and dressed as a mendicant. Arsh Taimuri describes his fate in Qila-e-Mu'alla-ki-Jhalkiya'n, translated by the author as *City of My Heart* (Hachette India, 2018): "One of the eunuchs employed by the Maharaja was from Dilli, and he and the Thakur appealed to the Maharaja to give refuge to the fakir. The Maharaja fixed an amount of two rupees a day for him, and Mirza Quwaish started living in a Sindhi's house. He would go away for a few months and then return to this house to maintain his disguise. He lived for thirty years after the *ghadar* in this way and became famous as Miyan saheb.

Hudson searched high and low for Mirza Quwaish but could not find him. Posters were put up by the British government for his arrest along with a big amount as reward. Tempted by this reward, Mirza Ahmed Shah Ibn Mirza Abu Saeed, who was descended from Shah Alam II; Ashraf Khan, a royal risaldar and a few others came to Udaipur many times. They managed to track down his house, but thanks to the kotwal of the city they could never catch him.

Mirza Quwaish finally died in Udaipur."

"Apaajaan, I can't walk anymore. Please ask the steward to send a palanquin for us," Naaz said tearfully.

'I started pacifying her through my tears. I thought my heart would burst with sorrow.

The eunuch said rudely, "That's enough. Get moving now."

'Naaz Bano was used to obeisance from servants. In her high-spiritedness, she scolded the eunuch, hoping to put him in his place. Instead, he flew into a rage and slapped the poor orphaned princess. Bano trembled with shock. No one had ever laid a hand on her. I cried, and the eunuch walked off leaving the two of us there. Somehow, we stumbled through the streets to reach the dargah of Hazrat Nizamuddin Auliya, where our family had taken refuge along with thousands of people from Delhi. Everyone was caught up in their own troubles and fears. No one spoke to the other or enquired after their health.

'When a wave of diseases spread in the wake of the *ghadar*, I was left all alone. Though peace eventually returned to Delhi, there was no peace for me. I lost all my family to the *ghadar*. The British government fixed a pension of five rupees a month for all of us. I still receive it.'

6

A Fast Amidst Starvation

When Delhi retained the right to be called the beating heart of Hindustan, the flag of the Timurids flew on the Lal Qila. In those days Mirza Salim (who was Abu Zafar Bahadur Shah's brother and had been imprisoned in the Fort of Allahabad, for some chance offence)[26] was once sitting in his *baithak*, meant only for male visitors, holding a frank conversation with some of his friends. Just then, a slave girl came out of the mahal[27] and said respectfully, 'Huzur, Begum sahiba is desirous of meeting you.'

Mirza Salim got up immediately and left for the mahal. After a while he returned with a glum expression on his face.

One of his close friends asked, 'Is your highness all right? I find your face to be full of gloom.'

Mirza smiled and said, 'Everything is fine, it's just that at times my respected mother gets angry at trifles. Yesterday evening during iftar,[28] Nathi Khan, the singer, was singing and entertaining

---

26. Mirza Salim, son of Akbar Shah II and Mumtaz Mahal Begum, died in 1836. There is no historical reference indicating that Mirza Salim was imprisoned at the Allahabad Fort. His brother Mirza Jahangir was imprisoned there and he died in 1821. Since Emperor Jahangir's birth name was Salim, the two are often confused as being one.

27. Ladies' quarters

28. The evening meal eaten after breaking a fast

me. Amma sahiba reads the Holy Quran at that time and she was displeased by the noise. Today she has commanded me to stop all singing assemblies during Ramzan. How do I give up this recreational activity? I have agreed out of deference but am very restless and wonder how I am going to spend these sixteen days.'

His friend replied respectfully with folded hands, 'Huzur this is a trifling matter. You need not worry about it. Come to the Jama Masjid before iftar and you will find a wonderful atmosphere there. You are sure to find very colourful personalities and interesting people there. Come and watch the beauty of God's creation in the days appointed by God.'

Mirza liked the proposal, and the next day he went to the Jama Masjid with a group of courtiers. He found an amazing scene there. People were sitting in groups. Some were reciting the Holy Quran, the Hafiz, those who knew the Holy Quran by heart and recite it at night, were continuing with their recitation, some were discussing matters related to Islamic jurisprudence, while others were addressing questions about religion. Large crowds surrounded these groups and were listening intently. Some were engaged in personal devotions. In brief, a wondrous spiritual environment prevailed in the great mosque.

Kullo jadeed al lazeez, everything new is delicious. Mirza admired this milieu greatly and the days passed pleasantly. When it was time to break the fast, huge trays of food were brought and distributed. The royal palace sent many trays full of the most delicious preparations to the Jama Masjid for distribution among those fasting. The food trays numbered in the thousands as apart from the Qila itself, separate trays were sent by the various begums of the Lal Qila and nobles of the city. Every noble wanted their trays to be the best and would send it covered with beautifully embroidered and decorated silken frilled tray cloths and these would add to the colourful ambience of the mosque.

Mirza was impressed by the spiritual and religious fervour that permeated the mosque. Its splendour and magnificence made him come back to the mosque daily. He noticed that hundreds of trays of the dawn meal and iftar were sent every day to various mosques and hospices of the city by his family. He liked the hustle bustle of these activities and felt that they brought myriad blessings for his household.

Mirza had a young nephew called Mirza Shahzor who spent a lot of time with him. When I asked him, Mirza Shahzor said, 'Those days seem like a dream now. There came a time when Delhi was ruined. The Qila was destroyed, nobles were hanged to death, their houses were looted, their ladies started working as maid servants and the grandeur and dignity of Muslims was razed to dust. After that I had the chance to visit the Jama Masjid during the month of Ramzan. What did I see! There were *chulha*s, wood stoves, built all over the courtyard and the soldiers were cooking *roti*s, flatbread, on them. Horses were being fed, heaps of grass bundles were stacked against a wall and Shah Jahan's beautiful and unparalleled mosque looked like a stable. After the mosque was restored to the Muslims, I once again went to the Masjid in the month of Ramzan and found a few Muslims dressed in soiled and patched clothes sitting around. A few were reciting the Holy Quran, while the rest were praying. When it was time to break the fast, someone distributed a few dates and some *dal-sev*, savouries, while another was sharing portions of a cooked vegetable dish. The food and hustle bustle of yore was missing and it seemed as if the oppressed of the world had gathered here.

'In our present time, Muslims have been completely suppressed. The English educated Muslims are rarely seen entering a mosque. What lustre can the poor people bring? But we must be grateful that people are still coming to the mosque. If the Muslim's state of impoverishment continue, God only knows what will happen in the future.'

Mirza Shahzor's words were filled with anguish. They had a deep effect on me. One day, I asked him to narrate the stories of the *ghadar* and the destruction that it brought in its wake. His eyes welled up with tears and he asked to be excused from reliving those painful memories. However, when I insisted, he told me his heart-rending story.

'When the British forces prevailed over us and snatched away the swords from our hands, divested us of our crowns, and captured the throne, the city was lit up by the cannon fire. The women who stayed behind seven veils were forced to come out into the city and find the writhing corpses of their husbands, fathers, sons and brothers. Young, orphaned children were running around calling out for their fathers. Huzur Zill-e Subhani left the Qila and went to Humayun's tomb. That day, I too left the Qila as the leader of a ruined caravan that carried my old mother, pregnant wife and young sister.

'Seated in two *rath*s, we were headed for Ghaziabad. But we had to turn back from Shahadra on hearing that the British forces had surrounded that area. We made it to Qutub sahib in Mehrauli where we rested at night before setting off further. Near Chattarpur we were looted by the Gujjars who took everything from us but mercifully left us alive. That deserted jungle and three women in my care: one an old woman who could not walk because of her infirmity, the other pregnant and the third an innocent ten-year-old! Thinking about the misfortune that had fallen upon us, the women kept wailing through the night. My heart was overwrought by the pain in their voices.

My mother repeatedly said, "O Lord where do we go now? Whom do we look towards for help? Our empire has been destroyed and crown snatched away. Praise be yours for giving us at least a torn sackcloth and a place to rest peacefully. Where do I sit with this sick and pregnant woman? Whom do I hand over this innocent child to? Even the trees in this jungle seem to have sworn to be our enemies and there's no shade to be seen anywhere."

My sister stood looking at us with fear in her eyes. Her innocent, helpless face filled me with pity. Seeing a village in a distance, I tried to calm everyone down and encouraged towards it. My dear mother could barely walk. She stumbled ever so often and would then sit down holding her head. "May fate put obstacles in the path of those who overturned crowned heads that were ever-ready to help the weak. We are the descendants of Chengez Khan whose sword struck terror in the hearts of people; we belong to the family of Timur, the emperor of emperors; we come from the household of Shah Jahan who covered a grave with jewels and built a mosque of unparalleled beauty; we are the kin of the emperor of Hindustan. Why is there no place for us on this earth today? Why is it being disobedient when we are in dire straits and even the sky is crying for us?"

The hair on my body stood up each time I heard her wail. Somehow, we finally managed to reach the village. The Muslims of Mewat had settled in that village. They welcomed us and made us reside in their *chaupal*, the community building.

Some days passed. The Muslim villagers took care of us, providing us food and letting us live in the *chaupal*. But how long could they bear this burden? Finally, they got tired and one day said to me, "*Miyan ji* a wedding party is arriving soon and they will be put up at the *chaupal*. Can you please shift to another hut? Also, why are you sitting idle the whole day, why don't you do some work?"

"Brother, we will stay wherever you tell us to. We have no rights over this *chaupal*. When fate has snatched the Qila away from us how can we stake a claim on a thatched cottage? As far as work is concerned, I have myself been feeling very restless. Tell me what work I can do and if it is within my capability, I will definitely do it," I replied.

Their village headman replied in his rustic tongue, "How do we know what work you are capable of doing?"

"I am a prince. I can wield a sword and a gun with some dexterity. Apart from that, I have no skills."

On hearing my words, the villagers burst out laughing. "No, no here you would have to plough the fields and weed the grass. What will we do with your skill of swordsmanship?"

My eyes filled up with tears on hearing this. "Brothers, I don't know how to plough the fields or weed the grass."

The tears in my eyes made the villagers feel some sympathy for me. "All right then you guard our fields and your women can sew our clothes. In return we will give you enough grains to fill your stomachs," they said.

This is exactly what transpired. I began to guard the fields from animals that ate the crops and the ladies would sew clothes for the villagers.

Once during the month of *Bhadon*, when the monsoon strikes, everyone in the village fell sick and started running a temperature. My wife and sister also caught the infection. There were no medicines or hakims in the village and the people recovered naturally. But we were used to medicines and physicians and had a tough time. The season of monsoon brought a severe thunderstorm and rain, making the village drain overflow and flooding everything around. The villagers were used to these difficulties but for us it was unbearable. We found the situation to be worse than death itself. The water entered our hut at night. The cots on which the ladies slept submerged in it. I woke up to the sound of the women who had started screaming. I made the two cots stand up sideways and asked the ladies to sit on it. The water receded after an hour but the sacks of grain and all our bedding were completely drenched. My wife's labour pain had started the night before and she caught a chill. I can't describe the events of that night. Incessant rain was falling down in pitch darkness, our bedding and clothes was soaked, and we had no means to light a fire for warmth. We were frantic. "O god what can we do?" The labour pain increased and my wife's health started deteriorating. She died writhing in pain. The baby remained in her womb.

She had been brought up in luxury and the conditions she was made to bear after the *ghadar* proved fatal for her. She survived the *ghadar* but could not survive the life after it.

In the morning when the villagers heard of her death, they came and made arrangements for her burial and funeral. By afternoon the princess was sleeping in her grave.

The next worry was food since our grain was soaked and spoilt. How could we ask the villagers for help? They were in the same situation.

The village headman realized our dire situation and got flour worth one rupee from Qutub sahib for us.

By the time half of the flour had been used up, the moon was sighted for the month of Ramzan. My respected mother had a tender heart and memories of the past kept tormenting her. As soon as she saw the Ramzan moon she let out a long sigh. I knew she was remembering the past and said some words of comfort to her.

The first four of the five fasts passed comfortably but once the flour ran out, we faced immense difficulty. That evening we opened our fast with water even as pangs of hunger attacked us. My mother had the habit of wailing loudly in times of distress and narrating her plight, but that day she seemed content and was quiet. Her contentment helped me and my young sister bear the situation with fortitude. She went and lay down on the cot and slipped into an uneasy sleep caused by weakness.

The night went by in a state of uneasy wakefulness and bouts of unconsciousness. My mother got up before dawn prayers to recite the supererogatory prayers and the pain and anguish in her voice as she supplicated before God are beyond my powers of description. She cried, "O God what sin have we committed that we, who used to feed hundreds of indigent people during the month of Ramzan have nothing to eat today? We are keeping all the fasts. O God, if we have sinned and are being punished, what sin has this poor innocent girl committed that she has not got even a morsel to eat since yesterday?"

The next day was no different. We kept a fast even though we were starving. In the evening the headman's servant brought some milk and sweet rice and said, "Today, we had held a *niyaz*, the consecration of food, and I have brought some food for you all along with five rupees that were taken out as *zakat*.[29] We normally give goats as *zakat* because that is our profession but this year, we are giving out cash."

The sight of the food and money seemed like a boon had been granted. I happily took them in to my mother and related the words of the servant, thanking God for his mercy. However, I had no idea that while my mind had accepted our changed circumstances, my mother was still wrapped up in her notions of ancestral honour and respect. Her face changed colour and despite her starvation and weakness she blurted, "A curse on your honour! You have brought home alms and charity and you are happy about it. It is better to die than to accept alms. We may have been ruined but our ardour

---

29. *Zakat,* which is one of the pillars of Islam, refers to a certain portion of income that is to be given away as charity, and is usually donated in the month of Ramzan.

hasn't died. We who rode out to battle and conquered lands with our swords and took what we wanted or died defending our honour, are not meant to live on charity."

Hearing her words, I dissolved in embarrassment and shame. I wanted to get up and return the food and money, but she stopped me saying, "If this is what God has written in our destiny, what can we do? We will have to bear everything with fortitude."

Saying this she took the food away. We ate it after opening our fast. The five rupees were used for buying wheat and Ramzan passed off without any more hardships.

We lived in the village for six more months before returning to Delhi. Soon after, my mother passed away and my sister got married. The British government fixed a pension of five rupees for me, and I live on that.'

7

The Beggar Prince[30]

There is a locality called Kallu Khas ki Haveli on the road that goes from Jama Masjid towards Chitli Qabr and Matia Mahal in Delhi. Every night after dark, a beggar comes out of this locality and goes to Jama Masjid. Later, he returns. This beggar is very tall, slim, and has a sparse white beard and sunken cheeks. He has lost his eyesight. He is dressed in dirty, torn patched pyjamas and kurta, and broken slippers which he drags behind him. He wears a frayed cap on his long, tangled hair.

The beggar holds a bamboo stick in one hand and a chipped earthen bowl in the other. From his face it seems as if he either consumes opium or has just gotten up from a sickbed after months as his face is very pale and wan. He wobbles and drags his feet when he walks. Perhaps he had been afflicted by paralysis at some point?

Piteous Voice

His voice is loud and piteous. When he calls out in his loud, sorrowful and wistful voice, 'Yaa Allah, please provide me with

---

30. In the 1934 and 1942 editions the story is given in an abbreviated form. In the 2008 version, it is repeated at no. 7 in an abbreviated version and at no. 27 in a fuller version. I have replaced the abbreviated version with the full version at no. 7.

flour worth a rupee. Only you will give. Only you can cause it to be given. Get me flour worth only one rupee,' all the people in the market and residents of nearby houses are deeply moved. Though except a few, they have no idea who this beggar is, why his voice is so piteous. A few women say that as soon as evening falls this inauspicious voice pierces their heart; God knows who he is, who comes every night to beg and is never seen during the day.

When the beggar emerges from Kallu Khas ki haveli, he heads straight for Jama Masjid with the help of his walking stick, dragging his paralysed leg, walking slowly, his gait dispersing dust all over. After every minute he calls out, 'Yaa Allah, please provide me with flour worth a rupee. Only you will give. Only you can cause it to be given. Get me flour worth only one rupee.'

He doesn't stop in front of any shop or person, just keeps on walking. If some shopkeeper or person puts some money, flour or any food item in his bowl he says, 'Bless you, may God never put you through bad times', and continues walking. Because of his visual handicap he cannot see his benefactor and whether he received money or food.

On reaching Jama Masjid he turns back and returns to the haveli, giving the same call on his way back too. Kallu Khas ki Haveli is home to many poor Muslims who live in small houses inside the compound, and one small and dilapidated house belongs to this beggar. He opens the latch and enters into the tiny house with a small room, veranda and a toilet. A broken cot lies in a corner of the veranda with an old worn out blanket spread on the floor.

The Emperor's Grandson

Except a few people, none of the Delhi residents know that he is the emperor's real grandson and his name is Mirza Qamar Sultan. Before the *ghadar* he was a handsome young man whose good looks and height were much lauded in the Qila. Once upon a time when he rode out of the Qila, the ladies would gather to see him and the people in the markets would stop to appreciate his looks and would bend to present their salaams to him.

Today, he has been compelled to beg because the *ghadar* of 1857 that resulted in the destruction of the Mughal dynasty and the ruination of Muslims. The government had fixed a pension of five rupees but his spendthrift ways meant that he pawned it all with the *bania*, money lender. Now he goes out to beg at night and lives on whatever he gets.

'I am the beloved son of Quraisha Begum, daughter of Bahadur Shah. In my childhood I was known as Sahib-e-Alam Mirza Qamar Sultan Bahadur. Today I am just a humiliated beggar. I was happy earlier, but even now I am content. How can one complain about the turning of the wheel of fortune?

'I was born in palaces and from the time I opened my eyes there were servants standing at my feet with bowed heads and folded hands. When I grew up, I witnessed a different scene. Nobles would run to obey my commands at just a glance. I thought I was born into this lofty position, meant to be feted and fawned over forever. I never knew there could be another side to life.

'May I be sacrificed over Allah's power. He showed us our place. We saw our rise and our fall. We enjoyed the royal glory and now we are experiencing the abjectness of a beggar's life. And both are unique in their own way.

'When the British fixed a pension of five rupees a month for us, we were Shahzada Alampanah once again. We borrowed on expectations and then drowned in debts. Now we must earn our own money, but how can we work for someone else? Meanwhile, I even lost my eyesight, and became blind and helpless. I was desperate, and finally took up the beggar's bowl. I go out in the dark of the night, when I can't be identified, and cry out for alms.

'People ask me why I don't come out in the day, but I am ashamed and embarrassed. How can I beg on the same roads where people once bent low to salute me when I rode through the streets?'

Mirza Qamar Sultan asks for alms with an aristocratic air. He doesn't address anyone, but just cries out, 'Ya Allah, please give me enough so that I can buy provisions for myself—*ek paise ka atta dilwa de*. I only ask God and spread out my hands to him and it is he who provides for me.'

He roams the streets of Delhi, then returns home.

Once someone had asked him, 'Mirza, are you addicted to opium?'

Mirza replied, 'Yes, I have got addicted to opium because of bad company and sometimes I smoke it too.'

If anyone asked, 'What all have you had to face since the *ghadar*?'

Mirza Qamar Sultan would heave a deep sigh and keep quiet. After a while he would say, 'Don't ask. I was dreaming when I suddenly woke up. Now that I am awake, that dream has not returned nor will it ever.'

(The prince passed away some years ago.)

8

A Family of Royal Descent

Hazrat Mehboob-e Ilahi would exclaim whenever he saw a delicious plate of food, 'How can I eat my fill when thousands of my brothers remain hungry in their houses? First feed a few of them, then bring this to me.'

When some new clothes were brought for him, he would cry out, 'How can Nizam wear this when his brothers are shivering, bare-bodied in front of mosques and open fires? First clothe them, then come back to me.'

Those who claim to be his disciples should first look after the poor.

Once, it was bitterly cold in Delhi. Water began to freeze in the vessels. Seeing the state of affairs, I decided to go and find out how my less fortunate brothers were coping. I went to Delhi to a friend's modest house, an area where many indigent Mughal princes lived. There was a small hut next to my friend's house where a family of royal blood resided. I had heard that the prince used to work in a Muslim trader's shop in Sadar Bazar, but had lost his job when the trader shifted to Calcutta. Due to his old age, he wasn't getting another job. The prince had three small sons and an eighteen-year-old daughter. The daughter was married but she had come back to her parents' house because her husband was not good to her.

I sat next to a wall from where I could see inside their house. There was a small store room with a small open gallery, and a small courtyard. The thrifty princess had spread out dried palm leaves on the floor. I don't know if there was anything inside the store room. There were some patched-up rags in a corner of the gallery. Three children sat on these rags wrapped in a torn and tattered blanket. The princess was cooking *bajra* rotis while the daughter was grinding chutney on the whetstone. One of the children called out, 'Bajijaan,[31] please give me some chutney, the roti is getting cold.'

The girl quickly gathered up the chutney and placed it before the children. They began to eat.

Meanwhile, the prince had returned. He covered himself in a soiled quilt and sat quietly against a wall. The girl asked, 'Abbajan, I hope all is well. Why are you sitting so forlorn?'

The prince looked up and replied, 'Don't worry. All is well. I spent the day pleading with people, but I could not get any job with which I can support the family. As I was returning home, I saw our [un] worthy son-in-law being taken away by the police in handcuffs. He had cut off a prostitute's nose. I was very saddened by this. When I came into our locality, the *bania*, grocer, from whom we take our provisions on credit very rudely asked me for his money. I was humiliated and came off wondering how to make ends meet. This bitter cold is adding to my woes. There seems to be no means of earning a living and above everything I constantly worry for you. I wish God would call me to Himself so I would be relieved of these difficulties.'

He bent his head and remained lost in his thoughts.

I saw that the father's words had a terrible effect on the poor girl. Tears flowed down from her downcast eyes.

This desolate household presented a horrifying scene. The helplessness and misery of the young girl had painted a picture that reminded me that life is full of both travails and comforts.

When the meal was over, the four children huddled together and the princess covered them with the ragged cloth lying in the corner. It was short, so while the boys could cover themselves, the girl could not. She had to fold her legs to keep them under the blanket. The

---

31. Term of respect for an elder sister

prince covered himself with the quilt he had been wearing and the princess used the torn blanket. That was the grand way in which this once 'royal' family slept.

I got lost in my thoughts about the vicissitudes of life. I don't think anyone would have seen a scene more loaded with warnings and admonitions for afterlife. If anyone living a prosperous life contemplated upon the life of poverty, they would never take pride in their material and transient possessions.

Tonight, I was suddenly reminded of that family, which deserves to be kept anonymous. Honestly, I wonder in a society where there is no food to fill stomachs or clothes to hide the body, how can one enjoy the pleasures that the world has to offer?

9

Bahadur Shah's Daughter

This is the true story of a female dervish who suffered through the travails of life. Her name was Kulsum Zamani Begum,[32] and she was the beloved daughter of Delhi's last Emperor, Abu Zafar Bahadur Shah. Even though she passed away a few years ago, I have heard her narrate her story many times. She was a sincere devotee of Mehboob-e Ilahi Khwaja Nizamuddin Auliya and was so attached to his dargah that she would often be found there. It was there that I heard her tragic tale. Whatever I have written down has been told to me by her or her daughter, Zainab Zamani Begum, who is still alive and lives in Pandit ka Kucha.

Here is her story in her own words:

'The night my Babajan lost his empire and the end was near, the Lal Qila was in a tumult. The very walls seemed to be weeping. The pearly white marble palaces had been blackened by soot from the gunfire and cannon shots blowing over our heads for the past four months. No one had eaten for a day and a half. Zainab, my daughter, was only a year-and-a-half and crying for milk. Neither I nor any of the foster mothers were lactating because of hunger and the trouble

---

32. Born in 1832 and died in 1902, she was married to her cousin Mirza Ziauddin Muhammad Bahadur.

brewing all around us. We sat disconsolately when Hazrat Zill-e-Subhani's special *khwajasara* came to call us. It was midnight and the pin-drop silence in the fort was occasionally broken by cannon shots. We were terrified, but since Zill-e-Subhani had called us, we immediately left our palace and presented ourselves before him.

'Huzur sat on his prayer mat with a rosary in his hands. I stood before him and presented three salutations. Huzur called me close to him. With great affection he said, "Kulsum, I entrust you to the care of *Khuda*. If fate permits, we will meet again. Leave immediately with your husband. I am also leaving. I don't want to separate myself from my beloved children, but I don't want to embroil you in my problems. If you are with me, destruction is certain. If you are alone, maybe God will open a path of escape for you."

'He raised his shaking hands in prayer and cried out to Allah, "Dear God, I entrust this orphan girl into your care. Brought up in magnificent palaces, my children now venture into the wilderness of desolate jungles. They have no friends or protectors. Please defend the honour of these princesses of the Timurid dynasty. Preserve their honour. The entire Hindu and Muslim population of Hindustan are my children and trouble surrounds them all. Don't let them suffer because of my actions. Safeguard them from all trouble." With that, he patted my head and embraced Zainab. He handed a few jewels to my husband Mirza Ziauddin, and sent us off along with Nur Mahal sahiba, the emperor's sixth wife, also known as Pyari Bai.

'Our *kafila*[33] left the Qila before dawn. My husband, Mirza Ziauddin, and the Badshah's brother-in-law, Mirza Umar Sultan, accompanied the three women: myself and two other ladies, Nawab Nur Mahal and Hafiza Sultan, whose daughter was married to one of the emperor's sons.

'When we climbed into our *rath*, it was dawn. Only the morning star still twinkled in the sky; all other stars had vanished. We cast a last glance at the royal palace. We wept and yearned for what had once been our happy abode. Nawab Nur Mahal's lashes were laden with tears and I could see the morning star reflected in them.

---

33. Convoy or group of travellers

'We left the Lal Qila forever and reached Kurali village, where we rested for a while in the house of our cart driver. We were given *bajra* roti and some buttermilk. Our hunger was so deep that the food tasted better than biryani and *mutanjan*.

'We passed the night peacefully, but the next day Jats and Gujjars from nearby areas came to loot Kurali. They were accompanied by hundreds of women who encircled us like witches. They took away all our jewellery and clothes. While these coarse women snatched the jewellery off our necks, we got a whiff of their breath which smelt so foul that it made us nauseous. After this, we didn't even have enough money to buy our next meal. We didn't know what was in store for us now.

'Zainab began to howl with hunger. A zamindar[34] was passing by and I cried out, "Bhai, please give some water for this baby." The blessed man brought some water in an earthen cup and said, "From today, you are my sister and I'm your brother."

'He was a well-to-do landowner in Kurali, and his name was Basti. He brought his cart and said he would take us wherever we wanted to go. We asked him to take us to Ijara, where Mir Faiz Ali, who was the *shahi* hakim[35] and an old association of our family, lived. But when we reached Ijara, Mir Faiz Ali was extremely discourteous. He refused us shelter.

'"I am not going to destroy my house by giving you shelter," he said.

'We were heartbroken and didn't know what to do. Penniless and homeless, we feared the British forces chasing after us. Those who were once eager to follow every glance of our eyes and obey even our slightest gestures had now turned away from us.

'And then there was Basti, who didn't leave our side and fulfilled his covenant of being a brother. We left Ijara and set off for Hyderabad. The women sat in the cart while the men walked beside it. On the third day, we reached a river where the forces of the Nawab

---

34. Landowner
35. Royal physician

of Kol[36] were camped. When he heard that we were from the royal family, he afforded us great courtesy and helped us cross the river atop his elephants. We had barely reached the other side when the British forces arrived and began fighting the Nawab's army.

'My husband and Mirza Umar Sultan wanted to join the troops and fight, but the *risaldar* sent us a message that we should quickly escape while they engaged the British troops.

'Fields ripe for harvest were in front of us. We hid inside them. I don't know if the tyrants had seen us hide, or whether it was unintentional, but the British fired a few shots into the fields, and soon they were ablaze. We ran, but we stumbled many times as none of us knew how to run. Our head covers got tangled in the grain stalks and we somehow managed to escape the burning field, shocked beyond measure. Our feet were bleeding, our throats were parched, and our tongues were hanging out. Zainab had fainted. Nawab Nur Mahal fainted as soon as we escaped the British. I clasped Zainab to my bosom and looked at my husband, wondering what was in store for us. What did the Almighty have in mind?

'It seemed there was no hope for us. From a position of royalty, we had been reduced to less than beggars. We didn't even have the peace that beggars do, as British forces and looters were hot on our heels.

'The two armies were some distance away by now. Basti brought some water for us from the river and we drank thirstily. We sprinkled some water on Nawab Nur Mahal's face. When she woke up, she began to cry. "I just saw your father Hazrat Zill-e-Subhani in a dream. I saw him in chains and fetters, and he said to me, 'Today, this thorny bed is better than velvet bedding for our poor souls. Nur Mahal, please don't panic, be strong. It was destined that we must bear these hardships in old age. Please give me news of my Kulsum's well-being. I want to see her before going to prison.' I started to wail loudly in my dream on hearing the Badshah say this, and then I woke up."

'She asked me, "Kulsum, do you really think our Badshah will be made a prisoner? Will he be sent to a prison like an ordinary

---

36. Older name of modern-day Aligarh

convict?" Mirza Umar Sultan replied, "It's just a dream, no emperor treats another emperor badly. Don't worry, he will be well-looked after." Hafiz Sultan, the Emperor's *samdhin*,[37] said, "These accursed *firangis* would never understand or appreciate the Badshah. They sell their own kings cheaply. *Bua* Nur Mahal, if you saw him in fetters, I fear they may treat him even worse." However, my husband, Mirza Ziauddin, consoled everyone and told us not to panic.

'Basti had by now brought the *rath* across the river on a boat and we set off once again. In the evening, we rested in a village populated by Rajput Muslims.[38] The village *numbardar*[39] vacated a hut for us. We were looked after very well according to their standards and given a soft bedding of straw which the villagers themselves used. I felt uneasy lying on the dry straw, but we had no choice. We tried to rest. After a day of turmoil, at least we still had our heads, even if temporarily.

'We woke up with a start at midnight. The dry grass poked us like needles. It was full of bugs that were biting us. I can't describe the discomfort we felt. In that moment, it seemed like our bodies had been set on fire by the bug bites. We were used to soft velvet mattresses. Even though the villagers slept soundly, we were in deep discomfort.

'We could hear hyenas howling in the dark. My heart sank. How quick is the turn of fate! Nobody would have thought the children of Badshah-e-Hind would be rolling on the ground in agony on a bed of straw.

'With great difficulty and after extreme discomfort and trouble, we somehow reached Hyderabad. We took a house on rent in Sita Ram Peth. My husband sold a ring studded with precious stones that had escaped the loot in Jabalpur. It helped finance our trip and initial stay in Hyderabad.

---

37. A relative through marriage: the mother-in-law of a son or daughter
38. Descendants of Rajputs who had converted to Islam
39. The revenue collector of the village, normally from the family of local landowners

'But soon the money dried up and we had no way to sustain ourselves. My husband was an accomplished calligrapher. He wrote down the Durood sharif[40] and took it to a few jewellers to try and earn some money. Whoever saw it was astonished at the artistry and beauty of the calligraphy. He was able to get five rupees by selling it. From then on, he was able to earn a steady income from his calligraphy and we began to live comfortably.

'But then, one of the Nizam's employees, darogha Ahmed, who had also put many houses on rent, suddenly switched sides. News spread rapidly that Nawab Lashkar Jung, who had given shelter to Mughal princes, had come under the sway of the British, and would no longer offer refuge to any Mughal prince or princess. In fact, if any Mughals were found they would be arrested.

'Worry began to consume us. I wouldn't let my husband go out in case someone arrested him. Soon we were reduced to starvation as the money ran out. Left with no choice, my husband took the risk of teaching a Nawab's son how to read the Quran for twelve rupees a month. But the Nawab was rude and arrogant, and treated my husband like an ordinary servant. He would come home and cry that death was better than such humiliation. "Until yesterday, men like this Nawab were our servants, and today he dares to humiliate me," he said.

'Meanwhile, someone had informed Miyan Nizamuddin about our presence. He was the son of Kale Miyan Sahib Chisti Nizami Fakhri, the pir of the Badshah-e Delhi. He came to our house in the darkness of night and his heart filled with regret when he saw the state we were living in. There was a time when Miyan would be seated on velvet and satin masnads at the Qila. Badshah Begum would serve him in person. But when he came to our house, we didn't even have a sackcloth that wasn't tattered to offer to him. He sat with us for some time and asked us about our experiences. Then he left quietly.

'In the morning, we received a message that he had made arrangements for a Hajj pilgrimage, and we should all leave immediately. We were thrilled at this news and started preparing

---

40. Invocations complimenting Prophet Muhammad and his family

for our journey to Makkah-e-Moazama.[41] We came to Bombay and gave some money to our true friend Basti and sent him back home.

'Aboard the ship, whoever heard that we were the Shah-e Hind's family, rushed to meet us. We were all dressed in the clothes of dervishes. One Hindu, who owned a shop in Aden and had no idea who we were, asked us which sect of faqirs we belonged to. The question inflamed our wounded hearts. I replied, "We are the disciples of the Mazloom Shah Guru. He was our father and our guru. Sinners have snatched away his crown and separated us from him, exiling us into the wilderness. Now he longs for us, while we are restless and yearning for a glimpse of his face. What more can we say about our *faqeeri*."

'When the Hindu heard our real story from the other passengers he started crying and said to us, "Bahadur Shah was our father and guru but what could we do? It was Lord Ram's will, and an innocent man was destroyed."

'Allah had made special arrangements for us in Mecca. I had a slave named Abdul Qadir, whom I had freed and sent to Mecca, where he flourished and was appointed *darogha* of Zamzam. As soon as he heard of our arrival, he rushed to meet us. He fell at my feet and wept for ages. He had a very comfortable and luxurious house, and he took us in. A few days later, the ambassador of the Sultan of Turkey in Makkah heard about us and came to meet us. Someone had told him that the daughter of the Emperor of Dehli was living at the *darogha*'s house and that she talked to others without wearing a hijab. The ambassador requested a meeting with me via Abdul Qadir and I accepted it. The next day the ambassador came to our house and was extremely respectful and courteous to us in his conversation. In the end he said that he wants to inform his master the Sultan about our arrival in Mecca. I replied insouciantly, 'We were now in the durbar of the biggest Sultan. We were no longer worried about any other Sultan.'

'The ambassador fixed a suitable amount for our expenses and we lived there for nine years. Thereafter, we spent a year in Baghdad

---

41. The glorious and holy city of Makkah (Mecca)

sharif, and a year in Najaf and Karbala-e Mo'alla. But we began to long for Delhi, and we decided to return to our city.

'When we came back, the British government took pity on us and fixed a sum of ten rupees a month for us as pension. I laughed at this amount. They had taken away all of my father's empire and offered ten rupees as compensation.

'But then I remembered, this land belongs to God and He gives it to whoever He wants and takes it as He pleases. Man has no role in these decisions.'

10

The Orphan Prince's Miserable Eid

This is a story of Eid from 1332 AH (1913 CE). No moon was sighted on the 29th Ramzan in Delhi. The tailors were happy that they had got one more day to finish their work. The shoe sellers were glad that they had got a bonus day to sell their wares. However, in a poor Muslim locality a Timurid family was surrounded by sorrow. They had just returned after burying the head of their family, Mirza Dildar Shah, that afternoon.

Mirza Dildar Shah had been ailing for the past ten days. He used to get a pension of five rupees a month from the British government. He and his wife made embroidered lace, and that earned them enough income to live comfortably. They had four children, three daughters and a son. The two elder daughters were married. A ten-year-old son and a one-and-a-half-year-old daughter were still dependent on them. Dildar Shah was very fond of his son. His wife was keen to send the boy to a school but the over-indulgent father could not bear to be separated from his son and refused to send him anywhere.

The thoroughly-spoilt boy spent his time loitering in the streets. He had learnt to abuse everyone. His Babajan was amused by this behaviour and never rebuked him.

Mirza Dildar Shah was a close relative of the Emperor Bahadur Shah. He was 65 when he passed away. Children born in old age, especially a son, are always indulged and spoilt. Dildar Shah was 55 years old when this boy was born. The father was besotted with his son and considered nothing too much as far as the son was concerned.

One day his friend said, 'Sahib-e Alam this is the age for the young boy to go to school and begin his education. If he doesn't go to school now, then when? There is an age for pampering children. You are embedding thorns in his path with this over-indulgence. May God keep you healthy always, but there are no guarantees in life. All of us have to die one day. If God-forbid something happens to you, this poor innocent boy will have nowhere to go. At least if he gets an education, he can earn and look after himself. These times are very difficult for the old nobility. We should be prepared for the future. God forbid that a time comes when he has to ask strangers for money and bring disgrace to our ancestors.'

Mirza Dildar Shah was enraged by this well-meaning advice. He retorted, 'You are making inauspicious prophecies about my death! I am not that old. People live to be a hundred. As far as the boy's education is concerned, I don't think it is necessary. Graduates and post graduates are failing to find jobs despite their desperate attempts. My son has a delicate constitution and is always falling sick. I have no desire to send him to school and make his fragile frame the target of a master's cane. As long as I am alive, I will ensure he leads a luxurious life. After me, Allah is the provider. He gives food even to an ant and provides for a humble insect living inside a rock. Why would He let a human child starve? *Miyan*, I have seen all the ups and downs of this world. Our parents didn't educate us, but we are still able to make a living for ourselves.'

The friend was rendered speechless. He regretted showing sympathy to Mirza Dildar and giving him advice. Then he remembered that it is a sin to stay silent when one sees some wrong being done. 'The one who avoids telling the truth is a speechless Satan.'[42]

---

42. A wise saying

So, he tried once again, 'Respected Sir, please don't take offense. God forbid that I should want you to die. I am only being foresighted. Please forgive me if you found it unpleasant or offensive. However, please understand that from the times when you were a child to now the world has undergone a sea change. The Qila was flourishing at that time and you were under the shelter of Jahanpanah Zill-e Subhani Bahadur Shah. You were free of all worries. But today there is no one to protect us. The monarchy has been abolished, the wealth has disappeared and only poverty and humility remain in the fate of every Muslim. Only those who learn some skill and can earn a living are prosperous and happy. Else humiliation and misery are all that they we will get.'

Dildar Shah came around. 'I agree with what you are saying, but most of my life has also been spent in these years of ruin. The government has fixed a pension of five rupees and you know how little that is! Our daily expenses are eight annas. We, husband and wife, make lace to make ends meet, and have managed so far without difficulty,' he acknowledged.

They were still discussing this when a third person came and joined them. 'The heir of the Austrian king has been killed. When this news reached the king he screamed in anguish, saying "God help me, the oppressors have robbed me off everything. There is nothing left for me,"' he said.

Dildar Shah burst out laughing, 'Bhai waah! This is indeed some next level of courage! He has been shaken up so badly by his son's sudden death. When Bahadur Shah Hazrat's sons, Mirza Abu Bakr and others, were shot dead and their severed heads were presented to the old emperor in a tray, he said with great fortitude, 'Praise be to God, we have triumphed. Men of faith and courage rear their sons for just such a day.'

The man who had shared the news from Austria asked Dildar Shah, '*Janab*, how old were you at the time of the *ghadar*?'

Mirza Dildar Shah replied, 'I was around 14-15 years old at that time. I remember everything clearly. Babajan was taking us to Ghaziabad when we were caught by the British forces near the Hindon river. My mother and younger sister started screaming and wailing loudly. My father asked them to quieten and snatched a sword from a soldier to defend us. Soldiers charged upon us from every corner the moment they spotted the sword in his hand. My father injured a few people but he was attacked by so many swords and lances that he fell down, fatally injured. His body almost in pieces. After his martyrdom, the soldiers tore the earrings from my sister and mother's ears and looted all our possessions. They imprisoned me and took them with me.

'When they were wrenching me away from my mother, her cries shook the very foundation of the sky. She howled, "Please leave my darling son behind. You have already slain my husband mercilessly, have pity on this poor orphan. How will I spend my widowhood? Who will look after me? Ya Allah! My heart will burst. Someone please ask Akbar or Shah Jahan to come from their graves and see the distress of this destitute and helpless woman from their family. Someone should tell them my story. See, they are crushing this piece of my heart callously. *Arrey*, someone save this flower that I have nurtured with so much love and care." My younger sister too ran around appealing to the soldiers to let go of me but it was of no avail. The soldiers rode off, with me tied to the horse with a rope. My sister ran after us calling out to me, "*Aakaa bhai, Aakaa bhai!*" But their pleas were useless. I was dragged willy-nilly behind the Britisher's horse. My feet were bloodied, my knees scraped. My heart was in my mouth and I thought I was about to die.'

'But Mirza, what happened to your mother and sister?' the man asked.

Mirza replied, 'Till date I don't know what happened to them after I was taken and where they could be. The soldiers took me to Delhi and from there to Indore. They made me work as a stable hand. Rubbing the horses and clearing their dung was my job. In a few years, I was allowed to leave. I took up a job as a *durban* in a Thakur's house in Indore where I spent many years. Then, I returned to Delhi and submitted an application to the British government. Like for some of the other royals, they kindly fixed a pension of five rupees per month. I got married a few years later and we were blessed with these children.'

Mirza Dildar Shah fell sick a few days after this episode. He left for the hereafter after an illness of ten days.

His death enormously affected his wife and son. Even though the ten-year-old understood that his father had died, he would still plead, 'Mother, please get my Abbajan back.'

They fell asleep crying. When Begum sahiba got up for *sehri*, the pre-dawn Ramzan meal, she found that her house had been swept clean. Thieves had stolen all their clothes, utensils, whatever little furniture they had, and even the meagre meal that she had cooked for *sehri*.

The poor widow started wailing, 'What will I do? As soon as my guardian's eyes were closed, thieves looted my house. We are left with nothing now.'

The neighbours gathered around and expressed their sorrow at this turn of events. A neighbour who sold *gota*, golden or silver lace, sent them milk and some bread for their *sehri*. The poor widow ate it with gratitude.

This was the first time that the widowed princess ate food given in charity, and it was a terrible blow to her pride. It was the day of the last fast in the month of Ramzan, and every house was bustling with preparations for Eid, except Mirza Dildar Shah's. The moon was sighted and the *chand-raat*, the night before Eid, was being spent by everyone in getting ready for the festival. But the poor widow was trying to console her orphaned son who wanted new shoes and clothes. She took the child in her lap and said, 'Son, your father has gone to a strange land. When he returns, I will ask him to bring clothes for you. See, your brother-in-law has also gone to Banaras. Had he been here I could have sent him to the market to buy clothes for you. Now, whom can I send to the bazaar?'

'I will buy them myself. Give me the money.'

As soon as she heard the word money, the poor widow started crying. 'Can't you see that thieves stole everything last night? We don't have a single penny left,' she said.

'I want it now,' said the prince stubbornly.

The grief-stricken mother looked at the sky, sighed and said, 'Wait I will make arrangements.'

She went to the window that opened into her neighbour, the lacemaker's house. She called out to the wife. 'Bua, I am in *iddat*[43] and I can't step out of my house. Please listen to me.' When the lacemaker's wife arrived, she related her tragic tale and said, 'For the sake of God, please give me some *utaran*, cast-off clothes, of your son. I will return them tomorrow.'

After uttering the words *utaran*, the princess started crying inconsolably. The neighbour felt very sorry. 'Bua, don't cry. Nanhe has many extra shoes and clothes. You can take one of these sets. Don't think of them as cast-off clothes. He wore them for a few minutes and then I kept them away carefully,' she said, handing over a set of clothes and shoes to the princess.

When the princess presented them to her son, the boy was once again happy.

The next day, the princess sent her son to the Eidgah with the neighbour. At the Eidgah, the orphan prince told the lacemaker's son, 'Look my cap is better than yours.'

The boy retorted, 'O go on you! You are strutting around in my cast-off clothes, wearing my cap. My mother gave it to yours in charity.'

As soon as he heard this, the prince slapped the boy hard and said angrily, 'How dare you say that we live on charity?'

When the lacemaker saw his son being beaten up, he came and slapped the prince hard.

The prince ran away in tears. The neighbour tried to catch the little prince, but he was nowhere to be seen.

The lacemaker returned home in despair.

Meanwhile, the orphan prince joined the crowd that was returning from the Eid prayers. A passing car hit him. The police took him to a dispensary to get his wounds attended.

At home, the mother was frantic. She was getting fainting spells as she hadn't eaten for twenty-four hours. She felt the sky was falling down on her. As if she hadn't suffered enough already, her son had

---

43. A period of four months and ten days that a widow or a divorcee must spend indoors before stepping out of her house or re-marrying.

now disappeared. There was no one to sympathize with her and go out in search of her son.

Finally, the lacemaker went and lodged a complaint with the police. At the police station he found out that the boy was in the dispensary. He went to check on the boy and then returned to relate the events to the princess.

Every house wore a festive look. The sounds of 'Mubarak ho!' were filling the air, gifts were being distributed and received. Every Muslim had decorated their house to the best of their ability and were celebrating with their family. In their midst, the poor starving princess sat alone and inconsolable in her house. She howled at the sky, 'O Khuda, where is *my* Eid?'

Far away, her son tossed and turned in pain, with no one to comfort him.

11

The Grasscutter Saint

Hazrat Deen Ali Shah Qalandar was a well-known, respected saint of Delhi. His sanctuary outside Farrashkhana is still famous.

Before the *ghadar,* as a young man intoxicated with youth, and proud of my spiritual lineage and wealth, I would often present myself in his service. I was conceited about my looks and very arrogant. I was the only child of my parents and my mother spoilt me greatly.

My father, Pir Ali, used to live in Khas Bazaar and had thousands of *mureed.*[44] Princes and princesses would come to him with their problems. The number of tributes and gifts offered to him were beyond count. We lived a life of luxury.

Despite all the wealth, Abbajan lived an austere and spartan life. His earnings as a gem cutter were used to run the household, he would not touch the money given to him by his *mureed.* One day I asked my mother, 'Bi, despite so much wealth, why does Abbajan keep cutting gems? *Khuda* has given us everything and yet he toils so hard. It's very humiliating.'

Ammajan smiled and said, 'Beta, he believes in the principle that he is a faqir who earns his own living and does not depend on others to provide for his needs. He feels that whatever his rich

---

44. Disciples

disciples give belongs to his poor disciples, not us. We should earn our own money.'

'So is the money that the *mureed* give him haram[45]?' I asked.

'It's not haram, but it is not our right either. It belongs to the poor. *Khuda* sends it to us so that we can distribute it among the poor, and as long as we are able, we earn our own living,' Amma said.

Durdana

Three days after this conversation, Nawab Zeenat Mahal Begum Sahiba, Begum-e Khas of Huzur Jahanpanah Mohammad Bahadur Shah, came to meet my father. A young girl named Durdana was with her. The minute I saw her, I was pierced by love's arrow. She looked at me coquettishly. However, we were helpless and could not speak to each other. I only found out her name after Begum sahiba called out to her. There was no question of me asking for her name.

After Begum sahiba left, I was struck by the pangs of love. I couldn't sleep for two nights and lost my appetite. But there was no way for me to meet Durdana. When my agony increased, I went to Hazrat Deen Ali Shah Qalandar and recounted my troubles.

He smiled but remained quiet.

I could say nothing more and returned home, hopelessly in love. On the way, I met the *patangbaz*[46] Hussain, who was my close friend. When he saw me, he asked, 'Is everything okay with you, my friend? Why do you look so pale and forlorn? Why are there dark circles under your eyes?'

'I have fallen hopelessly in love with a young girl called Durdana. It's a completely new feeling for me and I don't know how to handle it. Let us see what twists and turns of fate are in store for me in my youth. Will you help me meet Durdana or will I have to lose my life and end up in a graveyard, disgraced in love?' I replied.

---

45. Unlawful
46. Kite fancier

'Don't worry about such a small thing, brother. You can meet her through Naseeban, the porter. She often goes to the palace and will relay your message to Durdana,' Hussain said.

His words brought me peace. I decided to follow his advice and went straight to the Ghosi *mohalla*[47] where Naseeban lived. After giving her some money, I got her to agree to relay my message to Durdana. The next day, she brought Durdana's message that said it was very difficult for her to come out of the palace. But she suggested a ruse. If I sat on a spiritual retreat for forty days outside the city, she could bring the Begum sahiba there and thus could meet me regularly.

What an excellent suggestion! I immediately went to my mother and said, 'Lo Bi, you always complain that I don't care about my father's heritage and don't involve myself in religious activities. That I don't pray or fast. You say these are my days of learning and in case something happens to my father, this wealth of knowledge would go to others and we would be left to repent. Today, I am ready to obey your command. Tell Abba to teach me a few things. I will sit on a spiritual retreat near Hazrat Din Ali Shah's *takiya*.'[48]

'*Miyan*, I'm not ready to let you go into the jungle. Do whatever you want to at home. I can't bear to let you go away even for a second,' Amma said. I tried to persuade her otherwise but Amma wouldn't agree.

Finally, my father heard about it and persuaded my mother to let me go. He taught me occult incantations of the names and praises of God. A servant would bring me food from home for every meal while I was engrossed in my work.

Two Spies

After four or five days, while I was engrossed in prayers, two strangers dressed in old and tattered clothes came into my room. I asked them who they were.

---

47. Neighbourhood
48. The dwelling of an ascetic

'We are travellers,' they replied.

I was apprehensive that they could be thieves, so I asked them, 'Why have you come here?'

'We have come to take amulets from you. Durdana Bibi gave us your address,' they said.

As soon as I heard Durdana's name, a tremor shook my body. The night lamp was flickering, and in its light, I couldn't recognize the two men and wondered who they were and how they knew Durdana.

Finally, I asked them, 'How do you know Durdana?'

'We had gone to ask Begum sahiba for travel expenses and there we met Durdana. She is a very kind and cordial lady.'

'What kind of an amulet do you want?'

'To captivate someone.'[49]

'For whom?'

'It's for Prince Jawan Bakht.'

I was amazed to hear this. Prince Jawan Bakht was the beloved son of Begum Zeenat Mahal. After the death of the crown prince Mirza Dara Bakht, the British had made Mirza Fakhru the crown prince, however Begum Zeenat Mahal had wanted Mirza Jawan Bakht to be appointed instead.

'Who does Jawan Bakht want to captivate with his charms?' I asked.

At this, the travellers brandished their pistols at me. 'Don't reveal this to anyone. We are Jawan Bakht's spies. We want you to get the secret papers of Shah Alam that are now with your father. They contain the details of a hidden treasure. If you refuse to obey us, we will kill you.'

I got scared when I saw the pistols, but stayed calm. 'I don't have any problem obeying you as long as Durdana is ready to meet me. It seems that she is with you and that's how you came to know of these papers.'

'Yes, this is true. Durdana will come to meet you. We found out that *badshah* Shah Alam had made your father his confidant and

---

49. It was believed that with such an amulet, the wearer would be able to woo/seduce the lady he desires.

given him all the papers with information about the hidden treasure. He had instructed your father to give it to his worthy successors if the need ever arose.'

'So does Durdana stay in the mahal even at night?' I asked.

'No,' they replied. 'She goes to her house near Kashmiri Darwaza at midnight. We live there too.'

I asked them for the address of the house. 'I don't have any problems getting you the papers but I have no idea where my father has kept them. I have never heard of them in my life,' I said.

'Don't tell lies. The papers were being discussed the day you saw Durdana.'

I was extremely worried by now, but said firmly, 'Sahib, I can't do this.'

As soon I said it, they aimed the pistols at me again. But I was young, strong and agile. I leapt and snatched the pistols and began to beat them up. Both of them fell as a result of my blows and I quickly tied them up. I locked them in my room and raced off towards Kashmiri Darwaza. It must have been around 11 p.m. I went to the house they had told me about and called out.

'Who is it?' Durdana called back.

'Come to the door.'

When Durdana appeared, I said, 'I have been sent by the two men who had gone to the Shah sahib near the *takiya*. They have reached an agreement. They have called you there so that you can get the papers immediately.'

'Get me a palanquin and I will come with you,' she said.

I went out into the *mohalla* and fetched a palanquin. I asked the porters to take her to Khas Bazaar. I returned to my house after her and got her palanquin put down in a separate hall. Amma was fast asleep, while Abba was on the terrace. I woke Amma up and told her everything. She was scared but stayed calm on my request.

I took Durdana to another hall and lit the lamp. She was shocked to see me. 'Where have you brought me?' she said.

'See, this is now your house. If you scream, you won't be safe. I have imprisoned your spies and you are my captive as well. But my heart is your captive. I know everything now. If you stay quiet,

I will keep you here with your consent as my wife, or else I will kill all three of you.'

'I have no problem in living with you. My heart desires the same. But release those spies or all hell will break loose even if they suffer even a small scratch,' she said.

'If I release them, they will kill me.'

'Tell them that you can't give them the original papers but you can bring copies. But you have to do it in such a way that no one finds out you are in love with me.'

'I can't betray my Emperor like this. He trusted our family and I can never betray that trust.'

'Don't worry about that. Just write some made-up directions on a few papers. They have not seen the real papers and will not suspect anything. There are hidden treasures inside the Qila that they can't even dig up. They just want information in case they need it later.'

I agreed with this scheme. It was one a.m. when I went back to the *takiya*. I untied the spies and told them the whole story as instructed by Durdana. They said that if I give them the copies, they would help me meet Durdana. As they were leaving for their homes, I informed them that they would get the papers by the next afternoon.

The next day, Durdana told me details of false locations from her memory and I wrote them down.

Suddenly, Abbajan entered. I looked at my mother in fear. Durdana respectfully greeted him. Amma told him everything. Abba was shocked. 'This is terrible. We are not safe anymore. Our son had gone for a spiritual retreat, where did he catch this fancy bird? I will end their story,' he exclaimed.

Amma pleaded with him and somehow managed to pacify him. Abba saw the false maps and said, 'Bhai, you have really given them the slip. But that's good.'

I went to the house of the spies and gave them the maps. They were very happy when they saw them. 'If Jawan Bakht gets the throne, you will be covered in gold,' the promised.

I returned home, married Durdana and began living with her happily.

Ghadar

A few days after the above incidents, the *ghadar* started. My respected father had gone to a *mureed*'s house in Ambala. Durdana and I were with him too. While the *ghadar* was spreading, my father died in Ambala. We returned to Delhi alone.

We found that Khas Bazaar had been levelled to the ground while we were away. I took a house on rent and began living in it. All the *mureed*s of my father had been hanged, exiled, or reduced to penury. I had no one to turn to for help and had no ability to earn any money for myself. We spent what we had within a few days, and then we had no option but to starve. We had two children, and Durdana was a spendthrift. Finally, she suggested that I sit on a spiritual retreat in my old quarters.

In a few days, Hindu women started coming to me for amulets and charms. I would earn a rupee or more every day. I would provide them a protection amulet for five paise and an exorcising charm for five annas.

One afternoon, as I slept, I dreamt that my father and Deen Ali Shah Qalandar were talking to each other. My father was saying, 'I spent my whole life cutting gems, while my son is living off others.'

I woke up and began to cry. When I told Durdana everything, she said, 'It was a dream. If you don't do this, what else can you do? You don't know any trade.'

'I will find some kind of employment,' I said

I started looking for a job and a dispensary agreed to pay me ten rupees a month. Meanwhile, Durdana fell ill and despite every possible treatment, she didn't recover. When she passed away, I was grief-stricken. Apart from everything else, I now had to bring up two motherless children alone. I took them with me whenever I went to work. Somehow, we managed to get through a year.

The Maidservant

Soon I was promoted at the dispensary, and I started earning twenty rupees a month. In the evening, I would tutor two children and the thirty rupees I received every month were enough for the three of us to live comfortably. I decided to hire a maid to cook our food as I was finding it difficult to manage. While I was searching for someone, a poor woman wearing a burqa came to beg.

'Why don't you do some work? Begging is demeaning,' I asked her.

She began to cry. '*Miyan*, why don't you employ me? Everyone asks me for a guarantee, but where can I get someone to give me a testimonial?'

'Who are you? Do you have any protector?'

In between sobs she said, 'I don't have anyone except for *Khuda*. Please don't ask me anything more as I don't have the strength to answer.'

'Why don't you cook at my house?' I said.

She agreed and started cooking for us. However, she always observed purdah and never came in front of me. One day, by chance, I saw her face. She was an attractive young girl.

'This is difficult. I feel suffocated by your purdah. Why don't you marry me so that there is no need to wear this hijab?'

She agreed and we got our nikah solemnised with each other. After the nikah, when I looked at her, I found her face familiar, but I couldn't place where I had seen her before.

Finally, she said, 'Perhaps you don't remember, but as a child I used to come to your house with my Ammajan. I am the maternal granddaughter of *badshah* Bahadur Shah. My name is Gauhar Begum.'

I couldn't hold back my tears when I heard her name. God works in strange ways! This same girl had once been pampered so much. She was her parents' only child and would come to our house with great pomp and ceremony. I asked her to tell me about her trials during the *ghadar* and where she had been. The following story is narrated in her words.

A Princess Tells Her Story

'I was 13 years old at the time of the *ghadar*. My mother died during the mutiny, and I was living with my *badi dai*.[50] When the *badshah* left Delhi, my wet-nurse took me to a British general and told him everything about me. He kept me in his camp affectionately and, the next day, handed me over to a Punjabi Muslim officer, who took me to Lucknow where the revolt was still ongoing. The officer was killed in the uprising, and I escaped to Unnao, where a Hindu gave me refuge. I, however, suspected his intentions and ran away. On the way, I met a villager who took me to his house and married me off to his son. But I found it difficult to stay with the uncultured villagers, and life was hell. By God's grace, the villagers fought over a paddy field and my husband and father-in-law were killed by their enemies.

'I escaped and came to Kanpur, where I took up a servant's job at a trader's house. This trader's character was suspect. Though he didn't say anything to me, there was always a steady flow of women of loose morals to his house. I was horrified. I was desperate to return to Delhi. Somehow, I managed to get to the train station and pleaded with the stationmaster to take me to Delhi. He entrusted me to a guard in a goods train, and that was what brought me to Delhi.

'But once I was back, I was once again unsure about what to do and where to go. There were no familiar faces anywhere. I finally came to the Kucha Chelan where a porter known to me once lived. Although the porter had died, his wife gave me shelter when she recognized me. Her sons used to catch fish but had stopped bearing palanquins. I used to cook rotis in their house.

'One night the porter's son said, "These rich people have all the comforts of life. We catch fish in the hot sun and they live in ease."

'I said to them, "You get paid for your efforts. I'm sure those who pay you for the fish must be earning their money by putting in an equal amount of hard work."

---

50. Wet-nurse

'The older son got angry and said, "Get out. Who are you to interfere in our conversation?" He hit me with a stick and I fainted.

'When I came to my senses, I was lying all alone on the sand at a river bank. I didn't have the strength to move. A few Hindu women were going for their ritual bath to the Jamuna. I pleaded with them to take me to a hospital as I was injured. They took pity on me and sent me to the hospital in a palanquin. Once I recovered, I went to Sadar Bazaar, where I began to cook rotis at a Punjabi's house. But I finally left his house too as I realized he had designs on me. Then I had to start begging.

'One day, while I was begging, a boy came to give me some food. I found his face familiar, so I affectionately him, "Who are you?" He said his mother cooked rotis. When I asked him her name, he replied, "Ruqaiyya."

'As soon as I heard the name, I suspected she could be my paternal aunt and I asked him to take me to her. I entered the house and found that it was indeed my *phupijaan*. She recognized me too. She clasped me to her bosom and began to cry. She asked me to stay with her. I started living with her and helped her out for a few days.

'Unfortunately, one day there was a robbery at the house. Since I was a stranger who had started living there recently, the owner complained to the police that I was responsible for it. The police took me to the *kotwali* and punished me. One pulled me by my hair. I looked at the sky and cried in my heart, "I am the maternal granddaughter of Hindustan's Shahenshah. I am not a thief. Why are you tormenting me? I have no one to vouch for me in this world."

'The constable started beating me with a shoe. I fainted from this humiliation. I was finally let go by the *thanedar*[51] and started to beg once more—and that is when I met you.'

The Grasscutter Saint

When I heard my wife's account, I sighed. I wondered about the twists and turns of fate. We continued to live without thinking

---

51. Police officer

of the good or bad times. Time stands for no one, so we should not become arrogant in our good times or distressed during the bad times.

We lived happily for a few months, but then, I lost my job at the dispensary. I was fired over a small mistake. The children stopped coming to study. Once again, our conditions began to worsen. I started looking for a job but could not find one. People began to tell me that even folks with a BA degree were not finding a job these days and were roaming the streets.

I decided to go to the dargah of Hazrat Nizamuddin Auliya for pilgrimage. On my return, I saw a grasscutter walking past with a grass-laden horse. 'For how much do you think this grass will sell?' I asked.

He replied, 'Three or three-and-a-half rupees.'

'Wah, there is a lot of profit in this work,' I said surprised.

'But see the amount of hard work involved. I set off at 4 a.m. and have only collected this much by four p.m.,' the grasscutter exclaimed.

'Do you have to pay someone for this or do you bring it from the jungle for free?'

'I have taken a section of a jungle on contract for forty rupees and I cut the grass there. One section lasts for six months. I cut from different sides on alternative days. In eight days, new grass shoots break out, and then I go back to that area to cut. I spend eight annas on my horse daily. I have rented a house for three rupees, and the rest I use for my expenses. I don't have children, it's just me. If I had any children, they could have helped me cut the grass too.'

I came home and told my wife about this. She said there's no harm in taking up the profession as even the respected saints did it in the past.

I sold my wife's jewellery and bought a mule. I took a parcel of land on contract in the jungle, bought three shovels and, taking my children with me, started to dig up grass.

The first few days were hard, but slowly I started getting used to it. Now we can dig up a horse-load of grass before noon and sell it in the wholesale market for three rupees. I then go to the mosque and spend my time remembering Allah. Thousands of people still come to me for amulets and charms, and I give them away for free. They benefit from the charms and have started believing that I am a high saint who digs grass as a legitimate means of income, and they respect me greatly for it. Now I earn 75 rupees a month and I enjoy a better life than people with a graduate degree who can't even get a job that earns 25 rupees!

12

The Prince Who Drove a Cart

I

The Delhi Durbar of 1911,[52] changed the fate of Delhi. A new city was planned and maps were made. Renowned engineers stared working their magic. Many brick kilns were set up near the pride of Awadh, Mansoor Ali Khan Safdarjung's tomb, where the poor got employment. Once the bricks were ready, they would be sent on carts and trains to be used in the construction of the imperial city of Delhi.

On 11 May 1917, in the heat of the midday sun, an old man was carrying bricks from the kiln of Khan Bahadur Seth Mohammad Haroon towards Delhi. As he drove his cart[53] in the hot sun with

52. A royal court or durbar was held in Delhi in 1911 to commemorate the coronation of King George V and Queen Mary. They were proclaimed the Emperor and Empress of India. It was in this durbar that an announcement was made to shift the capital of British India from Calcutta to Delhi. It was held in the Coronation Park where two earlier Delhi Durbars were held. The durbar of 1877 had been held to proclaim Queen Victoria as the Empress of India and the one in 1903 was held to celebrate the coronation of Edward VII and Alexandra as Emperor and Empress of India. The park now houses the statues of many British monarchs and nobles.
53. The Urdu word used here *thela* means push cart. The prince mentions the use of the whip with which he controlled his bullocks, so that has been translated as bullock cart.

his grey beard and moustache covered in dust and perspiration on his forehead mixing with the red clay of the bricks, a motorcar came from Qutub sahib. The driver honked his bugle, but the old man was hard of hearing and couldn't hear the horn. He didn't move aside, and the car drove closer. At the very last moment, the driver swerved and somehow managed to avoid hitting the cart.

A fat Punjabi trader, intoxicated by his youth and alcohol, was sitting with a prostitute in the car. He saw an old, helpless man driving a cart and lost control. He carried a hand-whip, a fashion among young sprigs of the time. He got down from the car and started whipping the poor man.

The cart-driver was alone, old, feeble, and, above all, poor. But he had self-respect. After four lashes, he picked up the horse-whip he used on his bullocks, swung around and hit the drunk Punjabi with the wooden handle so hard that his head split open. The car's driver stepped out and tried to stop the old man, but was himself hit with the whip and began to bleed. The prostitute cried out in panic from inside the car, 'Please come inside the car, else this villager will kill you.'

Both of them got inside and started abusing the cart driver. The old man stood at the side smiling, and kept repeating, 'You are running away after one attack. It's not easy to face up to a Timurid slap, is it?' He was hard of hearing, so he paid no attention to their abuses and returned to his cart. The car went off, and the cart delivered the bricks to Raisina, where the new city of Delhi was being built.

II

The next day, two injured men and a few cart drivers were gathered at the Raisina police station. The old man was also present. The *darogha* asked, 'Have you injured these people?'

The old man stood quietly. The *darogha* angrily repeated his question, 'Why don't you speak, old man?'

A second cart-driver informed him, 'Huzur, he is almost deaf.'

A policeman went and stood next to the old man and repeated the question loudly. The old man replied, 'Yes, I have hit them. They attacked me and hit me four times with a whip and I gave back as good as I got. These rich people think they can trample us under their heels. Sixty years ago, their ancestors were my servants. In fact, I ruled over all of Hindustan.'

The *darogha* started laughing. 'He's a mad man. Put him in jail and present him in court. He should be sent to the mental asylum.'

III

Two days after staying in custody, the old man was presented before the city magistrate. The two complainants were also present. The court inspector read out the charges. The court wanted to take the defendant's statement. Since everyone knew he was partly deaf, the orderly screamed all the charges loudly.

'My name is Zafar Sultan. I am the son of Mirza Babar and *badshah* Bahadur Shah. My grandfather was the Shahenshah of Hindustan, Moinuddin Akbar Shah II. After the *ghadar*, I roamed all around the world before coming back to Delhi and driving a cart. When this incident occurred, it was 11 May 1917, which was as hot as 11 May 1857. I am almost deaf and could not hear the horn of the vehicle behind me. The driver and his passenger both did not take into consideration my age or the heat of the day and started whipping me. The blood that runs inside me has now become used to being abused, oppressed and beaten up, but it was not always so. From where the judge sits today, I have ordered the punishment of several rebels and criminals. My heart and mind haven't forgotten those days, even though my eyes have not seen them for an eternity. How could I tolerate being whipped? Yes, I took my revenge and hit these two "brave young men" on their heads. If you are ready to dispense justice due to civilized people, I am ready to accept with a bowed head.'

When the old man stopped speaking, there was pin-drop silence in the court. The European magistrate stared at him. A Muslim officer present in the court started crying. Both complainants were stupefied. The court discharged him honourably, and instead fined the complainants ten rupees each as they had attacked the old man first, while in a state of intoxication.

After delivering the verdict, the magistrate asked the old man with help from a *chaprasi*, 'Don't you get a pension from the government? Why do you do such demeaning work?'

The prince replied, 'I know that the British government gives a pension of five rupees a month to my family members, but I had been away from Delhi for long. It is also incumbent on me to earn my own living through hard work, at least as long as I can. I earn three to four rupees every day by carting bricks. I spend two rupees on my bullocks, my rent, and other expenses. What will I do with the pension? I am happy, I am content. There's no humiliation in being a cart driver. In fact, I am better off than those who wander around your courts looking for a job or spend a lifetime chasing degrees. I rule over my animals and am not anyone's slave.'

IV

When the cart-driver prince finished his namaz at the Paharganj Mosque, I[54] walked up to him and said, 'I was in the court today and heard a discussion about your statement. Can you tell me about the events of the *ghadar*? What did you go through?'

The cart driver smiled and said, 'Do you have the fortitude to hear me out? And can you believe the lies? I believe that whatever has passed, whether good or bad, is false.

'Narrating them again is like telling lies. What is yet to come is just a superstition; what has passed is false; only the present is the truth. I have come to think we should simply believe in the present and spend our time happily and in contentment. We should not mourn or remember the past or worry about the future, but live in the present that you can see and breathe in, and be happy.'

'These are your personal experiences. The trials and tribulations you have gone through have made your heart sorrowful. I am asking

---

54. Khwaja Hasan Nizami

you to recall your past so that I can note down the events of the *ghadar*. I have collected many such accounts and have written down the personal recollections of the princes and princesses,' I said.

The prince started laughing loudly. 'Perhaps you are a journalist. I am fed up with them. They all tell lies. But in any case, come with me to my house. I will not hurt my guest's feelings and shall tell you whatever you want to know.'

The prince took me to his house, a thatched cottage with two bullocks and a cow tied in the courtyard. Inside the cottage, a wooden bench was in the hallway with a bed beside it. A white *chandni*[55] was spread out on both. One could see the prince's refinement even in penury.

He made me sit on the wooden settee and went into the kitchen to get some food. He asked me to eat before asking him any questions. The food was enough for one person, but there were two different types of curries, dal, chutney and a sweet. It showed that the prince was living a refined life even amidst difficult circumstances. I tried to excuse myself, but the prince would not take no for an answer.

Once we had finished eating, the prince filled a hookah and placed it in front of me. Once again, I excused myself. But the hookah remained in front of me as the prince started telling his story.

V

'I am the son of Mirza Babar, Bahadur Shah's brother. Even though Bahadur Shah was just a titular head before the *ghadar*, he was greatly respected in every *suba*,[56] city, and locality. In Delhi everyone gave him the same respect and status that was given to Shah Jahan and Alamgir. I was a pampered son, and even though my father had other children I was my mother's only child. My father died before the *ghadar*. When I recall the day the rebellion started and rebel forces entered Delhi, the memories of their cruelty towards British women and children

---

55. Sheet
56. District

still make me tremble in revulsion. But soon the British came to
Delhi with help from Punjab and re-conquered it, and everyone
including the *badshah* fled. However, my mother was blind and
very frail by then. It was impossible to even get her on a *rath*, [57]
but I somehow managed it with the help of two women. We left
Delhi on a cart. The *badshah* and some members of his family
had gone to the tomb of Humayun, but I set off towards Karnal,
hoping to seek help from a friend of mine who lived there. A big
landlord, whom I would often meet in Delhi.

'Though my mother wanted to exit from the Lahori Darwaza[58],
we instead left via the Ajmeri Darwaza behind Fatehpuri Masjid as
the British forces were patrolling the other gate. We saw thousands
of children, women, men, old and young both, leaving in a state of
turmoil with boxes on their heads. The *rath* owner suggested we
should leave via Gurgaon to avoid British soldiers. Even though we
met some Gujjars on the way, we pleaded with them to let us pass
and reached Gurgaon safely. But we had only gone around two *kos*
from Gurgaon towards Karnal when a crowd of Gujjars surrounded
our *rath* and wanted to loot us. At that moment, a British army
regiment came towards us. The Gujjars fled on seeing them. The
soldiers came up to our *rath* and started saying something in English.
I couldn't understand it, but their tone was sarcastic.

'A *gora* then lifted the *rath*'s purdah on the side where my
mother was sitting and, seeing the frail and blind woman, laughed
uproariously. He said something to his companions and they all
rode away without harming us.

We progressed steadily until it was evening, and then stopped
to rest near a village. We had hardly laid our heads when I found
that thieves had stolen our bullocks, and the *rath*-driver had also
disappeared. I was starting to worry and tried to hire a conveyance
from the village. The villagers were Jats. Their *chaudhry* told us they

---

57. Carriage
58. Lahori Darwaza of the city used to lead east along the Chandni Chowk to the
Lahori Gate of the Red Fort. It was demolished in 1888 to provide easy access to
Sadar Bazar. It was one of the last points to be captured by the British during the
siege of 1857.

didn't have any spare conveyance but would call for one from the next village. My mother could, in the meanwhile, stay at their house.

'I agreed and took my mother to the *chaudhry*'s house. We had two small boxes with us, filled with gold coins and jewellery. The *chaudhry* settled us down in his house and sent someone to get a conveyance for us. But, a short while later, the villagers raised an alarm that the British army was approaching. The *chaudhry* hurriedly came to me and told us to run away, else they would be killed as well.

'I was agitated and said, "How can I run with my blind and frail mother? Please have some mercy on us."

'The Jat punched me hard and said, "Should we also die for you then?"

'I slapped him back. The other Jats gathered and beat me to a pulp until I was unconscious. When I came to my senses, I was in a jungle and my mother was crying near me. She said, "Those Jats put both of us on a charpoy and left us here in the jungle. I don't think there was any British army. It was just a ploy to loot our money and jewellery."

'We were in the middle of a jungle under the blazing sun, and there was no one around who could help us. We had no idea where to go, and feared being apprehended by the British. My mother said, "Son, gather your courage and let's go forward. There's more danger if we stay in this jungle."

'I stood up, and even though I was badly injured, held her by the hand and began to walk ahead. The jungle was full of thorny bushes. Our clothes were soon torn and our feet began to bleed. I somehow tried to prop up my stumbling mother but I couldn't do a good job as I was injured and weary. We hadn't eaten for two days. I would not wish such fate on even an enemy!

'My head injuries began to flare up under the midday sun, and I stumbled to the ground, unable to get up. My mother put my head on her lap and started praying loudly, "O *Ilahi*, have mercy on me, forgive my transgressions and save my son's life. O *Khuda*, this blind princess is entreating you, please don't disappoint her. We have no one except you in this difficult time. The sky and the earth have both become our enemies, and I have no one to call upon but you.

You can give respect or humiliate as you please. Till yesterday, we were owners of lands, elephants, horses and slaves. Today, we have nothing. I don't know why anyone wants to live in this fickle and transient land! Forgive my sins. Forgive my sins. Mercy, O Lord, mercy."

'My mother was still praying when a villager came towards her and said, "Old lady, give me whatever you have."

'My mother said, "I only have this injured son."

'The villager hit my mother with a stick and she screamed out, "O cruel man, don't hit my child."

'I somehow got up but couldn't stand for long and fell down once again. When I came to, I realized the villager had stripped us of our clothes and I was lying naked. My mother was badly injured. She was in the last stages of her life. I asked her, "Amma, how are you?"

'She said faintly, "Miyan, I am dying. I entrust you to God. I am sister-in-law to the Shahenshah-e Hind, yet I won't get a grave. Woe that I won't even get a shroud for my burial." Reciting the kalima[59], 'La Ilaha Illallaah Mohammad-ur Rasool Allah' (I bear witness that there is no deity but Allah, and I bear witness that Muhammad is the messenger of Allah) she passed away.

'I was in no position to dig a grave. I hid her corpse in the mud. I dragged myself to a tree and lay down beneath it, helpless. After some time, a sawaar[60] passed by and, on seeing me, came close. I told him everything. He had mercy on me and gave me his sash. I tied it around my waist to cover my nakedness.

'The sawaar put me on his horse and took me to his cantonment where he got my wounds attended to. Once I recovered, I started looking after his needs. He was a pious Muslim. He was from Patiala and took me there. I lived with him for some time. Thereafter, I became a mendicant and started wandering through various villages and cities. When I reached Bombay, I met a charitable group and left for Makkah-e Moazama with them, where I lived for ten years. Then, I went to Medina sharif and lived there another five years.

59. Also known as shahadah (testimony) this is the Islamic creed
60. An Indian cavalryman in the British army

Later, I visited Syria and Bait-ul Muqaddas,[61] and after visiting the blessed shrines went to Baghdad via Aleppo, where I lived for two years. I came to Karachi with a Memon, and from there returned to Delhi. I had been yearning to see Delhi again after all these years and had decided to come back.

'Once back, I began working as a labourer at the construction site for a railway line. I earned enough to look after my needs and saved some money too. In two years, I saved about three hundred rupees. I then bought a cart in partnership with another man. I was able to repay him slowly and eventually bought him out. Now I earn my living through it.'

I asked him, 'When did you turn deaf? It must be very difficult for you as you live alone.'

The prince laughingly replied, 'Thanks to God's grace, I have no trouble. In fact, I don't have to hear all the malice around me because I am hard of hearing. I lost my powers of hearing when I was thrashed by the Jats. I can still hear faintly from my left ear. The right is totally deaf.'

'Can I write this down in my book?'

The prince replied, 'Please do. But also add that everything that happens in this world, whether the passing of time, the mercies shown to you, or the troubles that oppress you, are all transient. They are all a warning sent to us by the Almighty.'

---

61. Al Aqsa Mosque, Jerusalem

13

The Mendicant's Gift

Itr and Two Eggs

You may love diamonds, or be ready to sacrifice your life for pearls; consider gold and silver the sum total of your life; and be besotted with shawls, brocade and golden threads; consider essential elephants, horses, palanquins, mansions and palaces. I congratulate you on these thoughts but there are such people in the world who consider these things transient and worthless and will not look at them twice in front of the bounties of afterlife.

God bestows his blessings on those he loves without considering their financial or social status.

This is a story of the time when the Delhi Qila was bustling with life and the Timurid emperor was alive and flourishing. One of the relatives of Emperor Bahadur Shah became inclined towards religion and became engrossed in worship of Allah. God had given him many luxuries including elephants, horses, servants and slaves but this devout man would stay away from these trappings of wealth in a quiet corner of the house. He would eat two *jau ki rotis*, barley flatbreads, morning and evening and drink water from an earthen cup and once again busy himself in remembering God. However, he was very fond of clean clothes and personal grooming. He had various types of *itr* kept in a small box. Every time he went to pray and be in the presence of God, he would use a different *itr*[62].

He had no attachment to any other worldly items and neither any emotional ties to his children, family or relatives. There were only two things for which he could lay down his life: the first was *itr* and the second was a pair of *sabzwar*[63] hens.

Once he would finish his devotions he would come out and give water to the *sabzwar* hens. He would look at them and alternatively laugh and cry. Perhaps he thought of the miracles of God's creation every time he saw them.

The Melee of the *Ghadar*

When the mutiny of 1857 occurred, all the residents of Delhi left the city; the emperor and his begums and even the princes left the Qila. This mendicant prince also tucked his prayer mat under his arm and got ready to leave. When the servants asked if they should take the jewellery and gold coins with them, he replied, 'I give all these to you all. I don't need any of them Allah is enough for me.'

He picked up his box of *itr* and two eggs of the *sabzwar* hens and stood up to leave. His well-wishers tried to reason with him, 'Sahib-e Alam, what on earth are you doing? You should take some things which will help sustain you. What help can these eggs offer? Money and gold can help you live your life.' He refused to listen to anyone.

He had one wife and a young daughter. He entrusted them to his servants and asked the servants to look after them and keep the two with them wherever they went.

'Take all the money and valuables in the house. It is up to you whether you use them for yourselves or on these two women. I don't intend to take along either my wife or daughter or hold on to the money.'

---

62. Personal grooming and applying *itr* is considered auspicious and a tradition of the Prophet.

63. A kind of hen with colourful feathers that laid hard eggs. It was used for egg-fights which was a popular pursuit in those days.

The Misfortune of the Begum and Her Daughter

The mendicant prince took his box of *itr* and eggs and went to the dargah of Mehboob-e Ilahi, Hazrat Nizamuddin Auliya, and started living in a ruined house outside the shrine. He bought a pair of desi hens and made them sit on the eggs and started his devotions. If someone gave him some bread, he would eat it or else stay hungry. Yes, he would use *itr* from his immense collection every time he prayed.

His servants took his wife and daughter to Gurgaon and started living on rent in a house in nearby Sohna.

For a few days the servants looked after the two women and served them loyally, but since all the money was in their hands eventually greed got the better of them and they ran away deserting the two royal ladies.

When the poor princess got up the next morning and called out to the servants, there was no one to answer her. When she peeped out, she saw that the house was deserted. She cried bitterly. There was no one to bring provisions for them and indeed no money to pay for them either.

The innocent princess was six years old and had no idea of the calamity that had visited her family in the past few months. She would get up every morning and ask for halwa that her mother used to get prepared for her. Now, there were no servants to make halwa or anything else. The princess started crying and added to the poor mother's woes.

The despondent mother called out to a neighbour who was a water carrier and taking off her golden bracelets and requested him to use them to bring some food. The water carrier's eyes glistened with greed when he saw the golden bracelets. He took them and went off to the market. He brought back some flour and sugar that could not have costed much. When the Begum asked for the remaining money, the water carrier said, 'The *bania* to whom I sold the bracelets didn't give me any remainder cash.'

At night when the begum was sleeping, the water carrier came and stripped the house of all their clothes and other possessions.

When the begum got up in the morning she started weeping and crying for help. The people in the locality told her that the water carrier had run away and he must be the culprit. She then told them about her bracelets. The wife of a *ghosan*, herdsman, took pity on her and said, 'Bibi, I will stay with you now, please don't cry.'

The begum had no other jewellery apart from those bracelets. The flour that the water carrier had brought lasted for a few days. After that she was at the mercy of the herdsman's wife.

One day the *ghosan*'s son pushed the young Nanhi Begum. Nanhi Begum's forehead got badly cut and she bled profusely. The begum had just this one child so she roundly abused the boy. The *ghosan* was offended and said, 'You are ungrateful and have forgotten our many kindnesses to you and your daughter. You live on our scraps and show us your temper!'

The begum was deeply wounded at this taunt and with eyes full of tears she said, 'Who are you to feed us? I am the daughter of that father who used to feed all the rajas and nawabs of Hindustan. Elephants would be tied at his doorstep; he was the guardian of the helpless and helper of those in need. Today I am ruined but my nobility and civility has not been lost. I will not listen to your taunts or be dependent on you for food from today. I can't sit quietly while your children hurt my little daughter. When God changes our fortunes, I will repay you for your favours and pay you back for the food that you have fed us all these days.'

The Serpent of Dreams

That day the begum was so mortified she could not swallow a morsel of food, while her daughter was moaning quietly from the pain in her wound and did not ask for food.

At night the begum dreamt that she had been swallowed by a serpent and that there was a garden inside the serpent's stomach. Her husband the mendicant prince was sitting in the garden and her daughter showed her wound to the father. The daughter cried, 'Abba, see how badly the *ghosan*'s son has hurt me.'

The father waved his hand at this and two angels descended from heaven. They put a snake around the girl's neck. The begum shouted out in fear, 'Oh my poor child.' She woke up with a start and heard knocking on her door.

She called out, 'Who is there?' The person outside replied, 'Your husband.'

The begum was shocked to hear her husband's voice and she opened the latch.

The husband came in and said, 'Let's go, the *rath* is ready.'

The begum asked, 'Where should I go and from where have you come?'

The prince didn't answer the question and instead picking up his daughter, gestured to his wife to accompany him. She went with him quietly. There was a *rath* standing outside which brought them to the dargah of Hazrat Mehboob-e Ilahi. He took them to a house there and ensconced them in it. Then he went outside. The begum saw that the house was well stocked with everything she would need. One small box was left open. When she went closer, she found that it had two thousand gold coins.

She was astonished. How did the mendicant prince come to Sohna and from where did he get these gold coins and other essential goods? After a short while, someone called out to her, 'Your husband's *janaza*, funeral bier, is ready. Please show your daughter the father's face one last time before we bury him.'

The begum was confused. Her husband had left the house less than half an hour ago. When did he die? She asked the man outside, 'Who are you and when did my husband die?'

'I don't know the circumstances of his death and don't worry about who I am. It was the last wish of the mendicant prince that his daughter should see his face one last time before his burial,' he said.

The begum sent her daughter with him and sat down with a thud in shock and grief. After a while her daughter returned and said, 'Abbajan has died. He has been buried in a grave.' The daughter hadn't even finished speaking when the man returned and called out, 'We have recompensed the *ghosan* in Sohna. Now, you don't owe them anything. Until this girl grows up, you will get forty rupees every month. Then you will die, and this girl will go to her husband's house.'

The begum fainted on hearing this. When she came back to her senses, she saw a maid servant sitting near her. The maid servant requested her to accompany her to Alwar saying, '*Miyan* had taken a house for you there. I will look after you in Alwar.'

The begum went with her to Alwar where she was taken to a nice house.

'The mendicant prince had a *ruhani muwakkil*[64]who was subservient to his every wish. Your husband passed away the same day that your daughter was wounded. All these things belong to that *muwakkil*. Lo and behold! I am that being and I request you to live here comfortably. I will serve you. When your daughter is married my work will be over. I had taken your daughter inside her father's grave to show his face to her as per his last wish,' the maid explained and then disappeared.

As promised, the begum received heavenly help till her daughter was old enough to get married. Once Nanhi Begum was married, the begum died and the divine sustenance stopped.

---

64. *Muwakkils* is a popular sub-continent concept. They are ambiguous beings sometimes defined as jinns or angels. They are made of half nur and half smokeless fire and at times become subservient to men who have done rigorous devotions and prayers to achieve this.

14

A Destitute Princess Talks to the Vicerine's Photograph

The young princess with her hands on an image of Lady Hardinge's statue asked, 'Amma, this statue is of this same Vicereine who has given me one thousand rupees.'

'Yes, my little one, this is the photo of the Laat sahib's[65] wife. She is very kind-hearted and always takes pity on the poor. This time she has paid attention to our helpless condition, too. Just give me this photo so that I may be sacrificed over, take all her trials and tribulations on to myself and lighten my heart.'

An Innocent Conversation

The young girl looks at the photograph and talks to herself.[66]

'May I be sacrificed over you; you are an extremely kind-hearted person. Your face has a spiritual glow that makes me want to sacrifice everything on you. But why have you come to the humble abode of us poor people? We don't even have two whole sacks to cover the

---

65. Viceroy
66. This seems to the translator a fanciful story based on a real conversation with the princess.

floor. Where can I seat you? We don't even have a cot and sleep on the cold floor. I don't want you to catch a cold. The roof of our house is sagging and I am scared that it may fall on you. What hospitality can I offer you? What can I put on the *dastarkhwan* for you? We haven't eaten a morsel of food for two days as Abba *Miyan* hasn't been able to pay off the grocer's debt. We are in great distress because of hunger. If I had anything at all in the house, I would have put it out all in front of you; I would have remained hungry but would have fed you, because of your favours on us. You have been kind to us at a time when the whole world has forgotten us.

My lady, I hope you aren't feeling unsettled in this dark and dank house for you live amongst light and glitter. What can I do, for today I can't even afford an earthen lamp or else I would have lit that for your comfort.

Where can I offer you a bed to spend this long night? All we have are two torn blankets, one of which is used by Abba *Miyan* and the other by Amma, with whom I sleep.

My dear Laat sahib's begum, please glance at my hands and face. They are parched and blistered due to the extreme cold. Winter nights are long and seem never ending. A good night's sleep is no longer in our fate. You have given us a thousand rupees and I will pray a thousand times to ward off every evil from you.

Amma says that once we were also well-off and we used to give away thousands of rupees in charity. Our houses had woollen carpets and velvet spreads, silk golden curtains and ceilings made of gold and silver were studded with precious stones. We owned shawls, servants and palaces.

Our ancestors were the sovereigns of Hindustan. People would stand with bowed heads in front of us. Rulers and princes would wait for a single gesture from us, and camphor candles would be lit in our mansions. We would take pity on the poor and helpless. We would donate generously.

When we went out in a procession, the runners would announce our arrival while elephants swayed to the beat of the drummers accompanying us. We had crowns on our heads; swords would be lowered at our feet and cannons would rain fire on our single nod.

Begum, where is that time now? Time waits for no one and the ever-shifting sands wipe out the loftiest of mansions.

Oonche oonche makaan thay jinke bade
Aaj woh nang gor mein hain pade

Those who had lofty mansions
Are lying in dusty graves.

Itr mitti ka jo naa malte thay
Na kabhi dhoop mein nikalte thay

Those who stayed away from the smell of dust
And didn't step out in the sun,

Gardish-e charkh se halaak huye
Ustakhwan tak unke khaak huye

They were slain by the wheel of fate.
Their skeletons too are now dust.

Zaat-e maabood jawedani hai
Baaqi jo kuch ke hai woh faani hai

Only the reality of the Almighty is immortal,
Everything else is transient and momentary.

God blessed us with every comfort of life; as long as we were worthy of it, we lived a luxurious life. When our actions and deeds became corrupted, we became engrossed in seeking pleasure and became forgetful of governance and ignored the helpless and poor. We let ourselves be flattered by the oily tongue of oppressors. God took away all our wealth from us and gave it to others. We can't complain as we were given a just punishment for our deeds.

You are as old as my mother, perhaps older. Who else can I share my heart's burden with? Where else can I express myself?

God has now made you our protector. Please see that we are suffering from pangs of hunger. Our days of splendour have now been ground in the dust. My face can't even redden with embarrassment because poverty and hunger has weakened my body.

We can't even celebrate Eid or Bakr-eid as we have no provisions even on these festive days to satiate our hunger. While the whole world is celebrating and wears new clothes according to their means on Eid, we eat dry, left-over bread and wear patched clothes. Monsoons makes us weep along with the leaking roof.

The dogs of Delhi city sleep on a full stomach, crows go to nest after having satiated their appetites, even birds have a proper resting place, while squirrels live in magnificent homes. But the family of Timur, descendants of *badshah* Shah Jahan who built this city, go to sleep hungry; they can no longer have even one night of peaceful sleep.

The ones, whose ancestors built the Red Fort, don't even have a dilapidated cottage.'

Beggar Princess on the Steps of Jama Masjid

'Begum, you must have seen the Jama Masjid in the city of Delhi, which was constructed by my grandfather Shah Jahan. People come from far and wide to see it but no one has noticed a veiled woman, hiding an infant under her burqa, her patched pyjamas peeping above her torn shoes begging in front of the steps of the masjid. Begum, this is that same wretched, destitute princess[67] who has no one to take care of her.

My merciful Vicereine, believe me, it was her ancestor Shah Jahan who had this masjid built. Today she is collecting scraps of food so that she can take care of the mosque of life. I feel embarrassed to tell you that these thousand rupees are too little. What can a small bandage achieve when your whole body is wounded and bleeding?

I pray for the welfare of your New Delhi where lakhs are being spent to build roads and may your new buildings on which crores

---

67. Reference to her mother

are being spent flourish. May God reward you for getting the old buildings of Delhi repaired at great expense. Please repair the unfortunate roads that wind their way inside our body to an empty stomach and do something to mend our broken hearts. We are also relics of the past. People consider us living curiosities amongst the other antiquities. Help us too. Save us from extinction. May God repay you with abundance for this.'

The princess suddenly jerked out of her misery and wiped her tear-filled eyes and said, 'I am a lunatic to talk to a photograph and pleading before a paper image. But who knows, perchance, someone hears my pleas, translates them and conveys them to the god-fearing Lady Hardinge. In turn she tells her husband the Viceroy, the council members and the King and his Queen that along with the construction of the new city and repairing of old buildings, some grand measure should also be taken to take care of the progeny of Shah Jahan.'[68]

---

68. The author, Hasan Nizami, mentioned here that Lady Hardinge had heard this plea and had helped the poor princess.

15

The Real Story of the Destitute Princess

The mother of the little princess whose fanciful story has been written above, had to undergo many trials and tribulations during the *ghadar*. I am now writing down her true story so that it can also be remembered.

She says, 'I was seven years old at the time of the *ghadar*. My mother died when I was three years old and I lived with my father. I had a 14-year-old brother named Jamshed Shah, whom people mistook to be twenty, for he was very well-built. Abbajan had lost his eyesight and was housebound. A *darogha* and four servants were stationed at the entrance of our house and three maid servants and one *mughlani*[69] worked in the house. Hazrat Bahadur Shah was our grandfather and our expenses were paid from the royal treasury.

One day I started teasing the kid of a goat reared in our house, and the mother goat butted me. In anger, I heated the iron tongs and seared the eyes of the baby goat. That kid died a painful death.

A few days later, the *ghadar* started. After the emperor left the fort, we too left the city with my father. We were in a palanquin and Jamshed Bhai was accompanying us on horseback. The soldiers stopped our palanquin as soon as we came out of the Dilli Darwaza and wanted to arrest my brother. My brother defended himself with

---

69. Female attendant

his sword and wounded one officer. But he was attacked from all sides and badly wounded. Unable to hold off any longer, he fell off his horse face down on to the ground. Two sharp stones pierced is eyes. My brother died a painful death. His screams were heart-rending. Abbajan got down from the palanquin and felt his way up to his son's corpse. He too stumbled on those sharp stones and was badly wounded. He too died there.

I held on to my father and brother's corpses and cried piteously. But the soldiers took away all our belongings and arrested me. I had to go with them leaving behind the bodies without a shroud or hope of a burial.

An Indian soldier, who was in the Patiala army, asked the British officer to give me to him. He took me home to Patiala. His wife was very hot tempered and she would make me do all the house work and massage her feet at night.

One night I was very tired after working non-stop and I dozed off while attending to her. That villainous woman heated the iron tongs and put them on my forehead. My eyelashes were singed and forehead scarred. I started calling out to my father for I was too young to understand that the dead can't help the living. When my father didn't reply, I was scared of the lady's wrath and quietened down. That woman felt no pity for me and asked me to keep massaging her feet. I couldn't sleep because of the pain in my wounds and had no strength left to attend to her feet. But what could I do? I had to continue following her wishes in that state.

In the morning while I was grinding the spices, my hand touched my wound and the pain was so intense that I started writhing in pain on the floor. That heartless woman said, 'Get up you fraud! You are only doing all this to escape work.' She took a handful of ground chilli and put them on my wound.

I fainted from the pain and only regained consciousness the next day. I woke up at dawn to find the soldier putting some balm on my wound.

A few days later, the soldier's wife died and he remarried. His new wife was very kind to me. I grew up in their house and they got me married to a poor man.

My husband died after two years. I came back to Delhi as a widow since that soldier had also died and his widow had remarried.

I also remarried someone from my own community in Delhi. A daughter was born to me from my second husband. He used to get a pension of five rupees every month from the British government. That money is spent in repaying our debts and we live in extreme penury and deprivation.'

16

A Canopy of Dust: The Story of Gul Bano

Gul Bano has turned fifteen. May God keep her safe. She was waking up to adolescence and unbidden longings were coming to her mind. She was the light of Mirza Dara Bakht Bahadur's life, the former heir apparent of Bahadur Shah.

She had been brought up with great indulgence by her father. After Dara Bakht passed away her pampering in the palace increased, as her mother felt that her innocent heart had been greatly sorrowed by the tragedy. She indulged her daughter even more than her husband so that she would never feel her father's absence in her life.

Her grandfather, *badshah* Bahadur Shah was so fond of her that he ensured she never lacked anything. His favourite wife and chief consort was Nawab Zeenat Mahal, whose son was Mirza Jawan Bakht. The status of heir apparent was given to Mirza Fakhru after Dara Bakht's untimely death. However, it was Jawan Bakht who was the favoured child. Nawab Zeenat Mahal was conspiring with the British government to appoint her son as the heir apparent.

Jawan Bakht's wedding was celebrated on such a grand scale that one cannot find a grander spectacle in the history of the later Mughals.[70] Ghalib and Zauq wrote the *sehra 70*.

---

70. Begum Zeenat Mahal asked Ghalib to write a *sehra* for her son, Mirza Jawan Bakth's wedding. The honour should have gone to the court poet, Sheikh Ibrahim

The famous verses of this *sehra* are described by Shams-ul ulema Azad Dehlvi in Aab-e Hayat.

Ghalib wrote:

Maqte mein aa padi thi sukhan gustarana baat[71]
Warna Khuda na khaasta Ustad-e Shah, Zauq se koi adavat nahin hai.

I wrote something in the *maqta* which became popular,
God Forbid, that I start an enmity with Zauq, the emperor's ustad.

No one was given any importance in front of Jawan Bakht and Zeenat Mahal, but Gul Bano was an exception. The love and attachment that Bahadur Shah had for this orphan girl was far greater than what he had for Zeenat Mahal and Jawan Bakht. One can only imagine the luxurious and pampered life that Gul Bano had.

Zauq, but he was reportedly unwell. In the *sehra* Ghalib suggested that no one could write the sehra better than him, which was taken as an insult by Zauq, who complained to the emperor. A slight to his mentor was seen as a slight to the emperor himself. Zafar asked Zauq to write a *sehra* as well. Not one to let go of an opportunity, Zauq included these lines:

jin ko daawa ho sukhan ka yeh sunaa do unko
dekh is tarah se kehte hain sukhanwar sehra

Tell those who claim to be eloquent
This is how poets write a *sehra*.

Ghalib wrote his celebrated *qat'a-e-ma'azerat*, letter of apology, in response to the emperor's reaction. However, the egoistic Ghalib left no 'verse' unturned in adding insult to injury, using poetry as a medium to prove his supremacy and take a dig at Zauq's ancestry and the emperor's negligence of himself.

71. The actual verse referred to by Khwaja Hasan Nizami is:

maqt'e mein aa pari hai sukhan gustarana baat
maqsood is se qat'a-e-mohabbat nahin mujhe

I wrote something in the *maqta* which became popular,
A reason to ending friendship I want not.

Mirza Dara Bakht had other children too but he adored Gul Bano and her mother. Gul Bano's mother was a professional singer and Mirza loved her more than his other begums. Gul Bano was 12 years old when Mirza died.

Mirza Dara Bakht was buried at the shrine of Hazrat Makhdoom Nasiruddin Chiragh-e Delhi, which is located six miles from Delhi in the ruins of Old Delhi. Gul Bano would go every month with her mother to visit her father's grave. She would cling to the grave and cry, 'Abba, call me to sleep with you, I don't want to live without you.'

When Gul Bano entered her fifteenth year, her childhood tantrums lessened but her temperament was still capricious and very mischievous. Every child in the palace would seek refuge from her.

She would sleep under a gold canopy wrapped up in costly velvet and silk shawls. Her mother would say, 'My darling goes to bed as soon as the lamp is lit.' Gul Bano would yawn, brush off her hair from her forehead and say, 'How does it affect you if I sleep and waste my time? You are just jealous of me and scold me unnecessarily.'

The mother would reply, 'No, Bano, never. Why would I be jealous of you? Rest as much as you want. May God give you a peaceful sleep every night. I meant that too much sleep is not good for your health. If you sleep early, then wake up early too. However, you don't wake up till mid-morning. All the maidservants are scared to make a noise in case you wake up and throw a tantrum. What kind of sleep is this? You should involve yourself in some work too. You are now grown up by the Grace of God and will soon be married to go to another house. If you continue to behave like this you will have a tough time adjusting there.'

Gul Bano would stamp her foot and say, 'Don't you have anything to say apart from this one refrain? Please don't repeat it to me over and over. If I am now a burden to you, say it clearly. I will go and live with my grandfather.'

The School of Love

It was in those days that Mirza Davar Shukoh, son of Shahzada Khizr Sultan, started visiting Gul Bano. The practice of purdah or segregation amongst the royal family wasn't followed inside the Qila, thus Mirza Davar could come and go as he pleased.

In the beginning they maintained the relationship that they were born with, of cousins born of two brothers. However, later a romantic relationship bloomed between the two.

One morning, Mirza Davar came to Gul Bano's apartment and saw that she was fast asleep under a gold canopy, covered by a black shawl, while her attendants stood with the flywhisk. The pillow was lying in a corner and her arm acted as a cushion to her beautiful face.

Davar Shukoh started conversing with his aunt but his glance would continually stray towards the sleeping princess.

Finally, unable to contain himself he asked, 'Chachi, does her highness, Bano sleep till so late? The sun is now overhead, you should wake her up.'

Gul Bano's mother replied, 'Son, you know her temperament. Who is going to take the punishment that will ensue when they wake her up? There will be hell to pay.'

Davar said, 'Aunt, I will wake her up. Let me also see what she will do.'

Gul Bano's mother laughed and said, 'Okay, wake her up. She respects you, what can she say to you?'

Davar went up to the sleeping girl and started tickling the sole of her feet. Bano yawned, and tucking her feet under her, opened her eyes and looked towards the foot of the bed. Her first thought was that one of her maidservants was misbehaving and needed to be punished. But when she saw Davar instead, she covered her face in embarrassment and got up immediately.

Davar, looked at her with love and longing in his eyes and said, 'Aunt, see I have made her highness get up.'

As love between the two of them blossomed, they both started studying the lesson of *ishq* and discussing separation and union. Gul Bano's mother realized what was happening and put a stop to Davar's free access to their apartment.

Nine Months After the *Ghadar*

In one corner of the Dargah of Hazrat Chiragh-e Delhi, an attractive woman was lying on the floor wrapped up in a torn blanket, moaning with pain. It was a cold night and the winter rain was falling relentlessly; the breeze carried the droplets into the enclosure where she lay, drenching her.

This sick woman lying all alone, helplessly had a high fever. In a delirium she called out, 'Gulbadan, O Gulbadan, you wretched woman where have you gone and died? Come immediately and cover me with my shawl. Can't you see the rain showers are coming inside? Pull down the curtains. Roshnak, why don't you come and help me; Gulbadan seems to have disappeared. Bring the coal brazier near me and rub hot oil on my chest, my breath is getting stuck in my throat from the pain.'

When no one came to her help she removed the blanket from her face and looked around. She was lying all alone on a broken cot in the hallway. The rain was falling down in the complete darkness around her. Glimpses of her father's white grave could be seen whenever lightning flashed.

When she saw the grave, she screamed out in pain and longing. 'Baba, may I be sacrificed over you. Look at me, I am all alone and helpless. Get up and see that my fever is rising and my chest is paining relentlessly. I am very cold but have nothing to cover myself except this old torn blanket. I have been separated from Amma. I have been exiled from the palace. Baba, please call me inside your grave, I am very scared. Take your face out of your burial shroud and look at my pitiful state. I have not eaten anything for the past two days. I am lying on the ground and my body is bruised from the pebbles here. Where is my gold canopy and shawl? Where is my soft bed? How long will you sleep my dearest father? I can't breathe.'

In her delirious state she dreamt that she had died and was being buried in her father's grave by Mirza Davar who was crying uncontrollably and saying, 'Now, this is the canopy of my unfortunate girl.'

Gul Bano regained consciousness and she started writhing on the ground, by now in the throes of death. 'Who will pour a drop of water in my throat as I take my last breath? Who will recite the Surah Yaseen[72] as my breath leaves my body? In whose lap will my head be laid? I have no one except you, O Allah and I testify that you are one. Your beloved, The Prophet, peace be upon him, is my sympathizer and friend and the Chiragh-e Auliya is my resting place.'

Reciting the Islamic creed, 'La Ilaha illalah, Mohammadan Rasool Allah,' the princess died. She was buried in the compound along with all the other orphans and destitute.

She now lies under her canopy till the day of resurrection.

---

72. *Surah Yaseen* is a verse from the Holy Quran and often called its heart. Reciting it at the time of death is believed to lessen the torments of death and make the passing of the soul into the next world easy. Reciting it over the grave is said to benefit the deliverance of the soul on the Day of Resurrection.

17

The Misunderstandings
That Led to the Ghadar

Khanum ka Bazaar was a famous locality of Delhi, in front of the Fort. Famous artisans and craftsmen lived there. After the *ghadar* of 1857, this locality was dug up and now only a bare expanse of land remains.

One evening in April 1857, Muhammad Yusuf, a goldsmith by profession, was strolling near the Lal Diggi[73] when he met the Hindu employee of a jeweller. The employee said, 'My Lala has been given the contract to make a gold-plated finial of a temple. He has called you to check out the requirements so that you can make it.'

Muhammad Yusuf's father had been a famous silver smith. All the silversmiths living in Khas Bazaar and Khanum ka Bazaar were famous as Lahoris[74]. Even today they are called Lahoris. They used to make silver utensils and gold jewellery. This community also controlled the sale of weapons.

Muhammad Yusuf's father was an acknowledged master in making silver utensils. He had taught his son the art of gilding and plating.

---

73. A tank in front of the Red Fort, no longer extant.
74. Perhaps a reference to Lahore as their origin?

Muhammad Yusuf agreed to go with the jeweller's servant but asked him to wait until his evening prayers were over.

The servant waited while Yusuf went to a mosque, said his prayers, and returned. Then he took him to Maliwara where the Hindu jewellers lived. Yusuf would frequently visit the locality for work.

The servant asked him to wait in one of the lanes while he went ahead for some work. While Yusuf was waiting, four men came out of a house. They were well built, muscular young men. The servant accompanied them.

The four young men invited Yusuf inside the house so that they could show him the work that had to be done. Yusuf became suspicious because they didn't look like jewellers, but he gathered courage and decided to go with them. When he entered the house, he saw a Maulvi sahib who wished him *As Salam Alaikum*. Yusuf was surprised but after replying *Walekum Salam* he sat down on the carpet.

The Maulvi sahib said, '*Miyan sahibzade*, the gold-plated finial was just an excuse to call you here. I don't wish to get any such thing made. These men and myself are strangers to this town and guests of a Hindu jeweller who gave us your name. We have heard that your uncle deals in arms and is a frequent visitor to the Delhi magazine[75] and knows all about the goings on there. At first we had thought we would contact him directly, but we learnt that he is a coward. That is why we thought it more suitable to call you. We have heard you are very courageous. Eight days ago, you had a conversation with the jeweller's son from which we gleaned that you are very faithful to your religion and hate the foreigners.

'I keep this Quran Sharif in front of you. Keep your hand on it and make a vow that you will maintain secrecy and never repeat what transpired here. Also, promise that you will do whatever you are asked to do.'

Yusuf replied, 'I am scared of taking a vow for this is too big and sacred a vow. Please excuse me. However, I pledge to do your

---

75. Arsenal

work if it is religious or spiritual in nature, then I pledge my life and belongings to the cause.'

On hearing his answer, the four young men drew their swords and pointed them towards his navel and said, 'If you don't take the vow, your life is worthless for we will kill you immediately.'

Maulvi sahib scolded the four of them and asked them to calm down. He then spoke gently to Yusuf. Yusuf was part fearful and part impressed by the Maulvi sahib's explanation and immediately picked up the Quran Sharif and kept it on his head and said, 'I am ready to sacrifice my life for any religious act that you want me to perform.'

Maulvi sahib embraced him and said, 'We just want you to somehow gain access to the magazine officers and obtain their secret documents. We have come to know that the British are conspiring to destroy the faith of the Hindustani soldiers and have greased the cartridges with the fat of pigs and cows. When the soldiers bite the cartridges to load it in the rifles, their faith will be compromised. If this information is correct, then there will be some documents relating to it in the magazine. We need proof so that we can take revenge in the name of God. These four men are Hindus employed in the army and have been assigned to this work by their Muslim officers.'

Yusuf replied, 'Due to some personal reasons I don't visit my uncle's house. It is going to be difficult for me to reach the magazine.'

Maulvi sahib smiled and said, "I know that you are engaged to your uncle's daughter and that is why you don't visit. However, you don't need to go to his house. You just become more friendly with him and start going with him to the magazine. Then you can try to get your hands on the documents.'

Yusuf said, 'Even if I do manage to go to the magazine it will be impossible to lay my hands on the documents there. The sahibs there don't leave important papers lying around.'

Maulvi sahib reassured him, 'Don't accept defeat before you start. Once you start going there, God will give you divine help and we will also guide you.'

Yusuf agreed and left. He was trying to think of ways and means to fulfil his promise.

The Guard of the Magazine

Rahim Baksh was a guard at the magazine. He was also involved in taking care of the personal affairs of the officers. On the third day after Yusuf started going to the magazine with his uncle, Rahim Baksh called him aside and said, 'You will need my help in carrying out the work you have been asked to do. Maulvi sahib has taken an oath from me too, but I can't do anything directly myself as sahib has become suspicious of me. I can tell you that sahib's boxes, which contain the documents, are kept in the room next to the terrace of the *gokhuru*.[76] Sahib has instructed me to clean the *gokhuru* the day after tomorrow. Your uncle will bring workers for the task. You can accompany them and somehow pick the lock at the back and enter the other room.'

Yusuf was elated to hear this information. He had found a way to honour his oath. The next day he came with his uncle and started cleaning the rust from the iron crowfeet. While cleaning, he saw the door to the room with the documents. There was a huge lock on it.

In the afternoon when all the workers came out of the magazine to have lunch and rest for a while, Yusuf stayed back. There was one Hindu sentry guarding the room. Rahim Baksh sensed an opportunity. He came and told the sentry, 'A man just came and told me that your wife has fallen off the roof. Go to help her quickly. I will stay here and call another sentry to replace you.'

The sentry immediately left. Yusuf quickly picked the lock with the instruments being used to clean the *gokhuru*. He entered the room and found that the boxes were also locked. He tried to pick the lock once again but was unsuccessful. Finally, when there was no other option, he broke the lock and found that the box was empty. Yusuf quickly broke the lock of the other box and found papers inside it. However, the papers were so voluminous that one single person could not carry them. Quickly making a decision, he only took those documents which were inside envelopes. He

---

76. *Gokhuru* are iron crows' feet thrown on the ground to check the advance of a cavalry. The reference must be to the room where they were stored.

wrapped the papers inside a handkerchief, and relocking the room came outside.

When the workers returned to work, Yusuf left and headed straight to Maliwara where he handed over the papers to Maulvi sahib.

Maulvi sahib immediately called a man who had also been sworn to secrecy. He knew how to read English. However, there was no news or information related to the cartridges in the documents.

They found a letter inside an envelope which had come from Meerut. It mentioned a discussion amongst the soldiers regarding the new cartridges.

Maulvi sahib said, 'At least we know some suspicious activity is afoot and that is why this discussion took place.'

Yusuf said, "But there is nothing suspicious in this.'

Maulvi sahib replied, '*Miyan*, you are very young and don't understand the complexities of the mature mind.' He immediately started preparing for a journey, and after praising Yusuf for his efforts, left Delhi for some unknown destination.

The *Ghadar* Has Started

Finally, it was 11 May and the rebellious sepoys of Meerut came to Delhi and created havoc here.

The British were being murdered, mansions were being burnt, and there was chaos everywhere as loot and plunder was being carried out. Yusuf came out of his room below the Qila and recognized one of the cavalrymen[77] as the four men he had met with Maulvi sahib. The cavalryman said, 'Yusuf, come with us we have some work for you. We all want to capture the magazine. Come with us and see the spectacle.'

Yusuf replied, 'What will I do there? I am not a soldier. I don't have weapons either.'

---

77. Some of the cavalrymen of 3rd Bengal Light Cavalry stationed at Meerut had rebelled against the policies of the East India Company and come to Delhi to exhort the Mughal Emperor Bahadur Shah Zafar to lead them against the British forces.

The cavalryman forced him to accompany them saying, 'There will be no fighting there. All the British have either been murdered or are on the run. The Indian soldiers are all with us.'

After being reassured, Yusuf accompanied the cavalryman towards the Kashmiri Darwaza. When they reached the magazine, they found that the door was locked and the mutinous soldiers had surrounded it. After a while, Rahim Baksh peeped out of the wicket gate and said, 'Bring ladders from the Qila and climb inside. There are just a few British here.'

Yusuf came close to Rahim Baksh and asked him, 'Has anyone come to know of the theft of papers from the room?'

Rahim Baksh replied, 'These heedless drunkards are still unaware.'

The sepoys went to bring the ladders and Yusuf returned home. After a while he heard a loud explosion which shook the foundations of the city. It seemed as if the earth had split open and everything had been buried inside. It was the sound of the magazine being blown up!

The bits and pieces of cannon balls were pelting down from the sky like a hailstorm. Thousands were killed and injured. The sky was filled with smoke for hours and screams of the injured could be heard all around.

Delhi Has Been Won

After a few months of tribulations, the British gained victory. They arrived with the army from Punjab[78] and after a few bloody battles they re-conquered Delhi.

During the period when Delhi was being bombarded with British cannons and its residents were fleeing, Yusuf's uncle asked Yusuf's father, 'The outcome seems very bleak. It might be better if we solemnise Yusuf's nikah so that when we run there are no problems of *purdah*.'

Yusuf's father agreed and Yusuf's marriage ceremony was performed. The nikah had barely been completed when they received

---

78. The army supplied by the Maharaja of Patiala to the British to fight the 'rebels'.

the news that the British forces had entered Delhi and the emperor had left the Qila to go to Humayun's tomb.

Yusuf's entire family also left the city in *raths* and went straight to Qutub sahib (Mehrauli).

Yusuf had not even seen his bride's face till then. The place where they found refuge in Qutub sahib was in ruins and it was difficult for the family to survive there. Despite all the challenges of the trying circumstances, the bride maintained the decorum of a newly wed girl.

At midnight, while they slept, the British cavalry surrounded them and began to search Yusuf. The soldiers arrested the men. After identifying each one, they took Yusuf, his father and uncle with them and released the rest.

When Yusuf was leaving, his mother started wailing and crying. 'He is my only son, all that I have earned in the last twenty years. How will I live without him? He has only been wed yesterday and still has not seen his bride. Where are you taking him and why?'

One cavalryman said, 'He is a rebellious criminal and will be hanged. You can meet him for the last time for he will not return to you.'

Yusuf's mother shrieked loudly on hearing this and fell to the ground in a swoon. Yusuf's wife was still sitting shyly with her head covered. When she heard the cavalryman, she lifted the veil from her head and stood up wailing. Her lips trembled with grief and copious tears rolled down her cheek. She looked at Yusuf, silently with a yearning gaze and kept staring at him.

Yusuf was a stoic man, but on seeing his new bride's tears he was seized with restlessness and looked at his inconsolable bride with longing eyes. Both he and his bride were silent. The bride's *surma* had run down with her tears and stained her once rosy cheeks, while Yusuf's face was white and pale from fear and despair.

When the hands of Yusuf and his father and uncle were tied with ropes and were being taken away by the cavalrymen, his wife said softly, 'I hereby forgo my *mehr*.[79]'

---

79. Bride money fixed at time of marriage. It is an amount to be given by a husband to his wife.

The Time of Hanging

After an enquiry it was established that Yusuf and his uncle were guilty of being a part of the conspiracy to bring down the magazine, while Yusuf's father was innocent. His father was released but the other two were sentenced to death by hanging.

Yusuf saw the Maulvi sahib in the jailhouse where all these prisoners were locked up.

The Maulvi sahib tried to console Yusuf and told him that one of the four cavalrymen had betrayed them. Yusuf asked Maulvi sahib where he had gone.

The Maulvi sahib replied, 'I had gone to Meerut but later returned to Delhi. The spy had shared all the details of the incident with the British officers. Rahim Baksh was blown up with the magazine and I was arrested in Delhi.'

Yusuf's uncle told the Maulvi sahib about his daughter's condition. The latter replied, 'Undoubtedly, our circumstances are very distressing but we did what we did for the sake of our faith. We were convinced that the British wanted to convert us to Christianity. Now, I know that the British were blameless and false rumours had been spread by those who wanted to sow seeds of discord. However, our intentions were good and we did everything for our faith. God will reward us and we will become martyrs. This sin has been committed by those who caused the *ghadar* by spearing false rumours.'

Yusuf said, 'When you saw the papers you had said that they prove the deceit of the British. Now you are calling them innocent.'

Maulvi sahib replied, 'That is what I thought at that time. However, when I reached Meerut and we studied the papers in detail I informed the Indian army officers that there was no proof of the ill intentions of the British. But they refused to listen to me and the mutiny took place.'

In the morning they were all taken to the gallows. Maulvi sahib was the first to be hanged. He called out, 'Nobody should dare to lose hope. We are all victims of a misunderstanding. God will forgive us and punish those who committed atrocities against English women and children.'

Yusuf and his uncle were hanged after Maulvi sahib.

18

The Prince Becomes a Sweeper

It is easy to understand the difference between past and present by reflecting on the work of European philosophers. But only the mind can understand it as the eyes can't process what they observe.

From 4 August 1914[80], the 'today' of the Germans was in front of our eyes and no one could predict their 'tomorrow'. But 1918 demonstrated it, showed it and made us understand what the future beholds. And now, there is no need for philosophy.

The 'today' of Russia was famous for centuries. Every child in Hindustan heard stories of its arrival and perceived the attack by a barbaric, wicked enemy as an arrival of peace. But the 'today' has ended and the 'tomorrow' showed us that the monarchy itself was overthrown in Russia.

The reputation of the Mughals in Delhi was based on two diverse attributes: its military might and its lavish assemblies. No region in Hindustan dared to deny their pre-eminence and glory. But when their 'today' ended no one could bear to see their 'tomorrow'.

A Delhiite heard the stories of the destruction of the great Mughal dynasty from the members of their family and penned them down. The stories of their miseries were given the title of a masterpiece and

---

80. A reference to World War I : 28 July 1914–11 November 1918. 4th August 1914 is the day that Great Britain declared war on Germany.

they gained great popularity. That Delhiite thought that everyone was talking about his story telling and not about the stories themselves. No one had stopped to reflect on how they could learn from the true stories which were a warning to all.

A community on the decline makes the intent its purpose. Such is the state of Hindustan that those who heard the stories only paid attention to the style of description and to the writing, praising them but not understanding the depth of the message conveyed through it. Even if they did think of it, they did not consider it necessary to highlight the lessons to be learnt from them.

In 1917, I was sitting with my dear friend Mullah Wahidi, who was the editor of the newspaper *Khatib* and the magazine *Nizam al-Mashaikh*. He was sitting at his desk deeply engrossed in his work. His assistants were also busy with work.

I noticed a sweeper, busy sweeping the grounds outside and glancing longingly at the flowers in the garden.

When he had finished cleaning the courtyard, he took some water from the tap and started watering the flowers. His hands were moving tenderly over the petals and with so much love that I felt he was a nature lover. He cleaned each pot and pruned the withered leaves.

Just then, Wahidi sahib called out, 'Mehmood Jaroobkash!'

'Coming, sir,' he replied and came running. He stood in front of the editor with folded hands. As soon as he received fresh orders, he left to comply with them.

His agility, his etiquette and manners impressed me and I wondered to myself that not many employees with this degree of refinement can be found.

When I asked Wahidi sahib about him, I found out that he was a Timurid prince and a close relative of the emperor of Delhi.

The extreme agitation and restlessness I felt on hearing this was more than what a Russian would have felt on hearing about the execution of the tsar. That was the news of a death and it was over. This was the news of a life which I could not expect to end anytime soon.

After that day, I started remembering the sweeper by his original name Sahib-e Alam. All Mughal princes were addressed by this title while the dynasty was flourishing. So much so that even when the lamp of the Mughal Empire was flickering, the British officers would address every royal prince, however removed he was in the royal order, by this title.

Mirza Mehmood is a young man and he lives next to the newspaper office. He has young children who have perhaps not forgotten their former glory, for they look embarrassed when they see their father working as a sweeper to put food on their plates.

The children of a conquering race never feel shy of working hard to earn a living but on the condition that they have some hope that their condition would improve. Their life would be nothing less than hell if they lost this hope of regaining their former glory.

Timur, Babur and Humayun had seen the vagaries of time and dangers of the world, manifold times more than their descendant Mirza Mehmood. But eventually all lay in dust. Mirza Mehmood can't hope that his adversities would ever come to an end and he would be free of this lowly employment. Mirza Mehmood must hardly ever think of comparing his 'today' with his 'yesterday' or else he would have become a saint in a single day and people would flock to his doorstep with bowed heads to take his blessings.

The day that I came to know of Mirza Mehmood, Wahidi sahib told me that one of the workers in his printing press was the grandson of Hazrat Maulana Shah Abdul Aziz Mohaddis-e Delhi. I felt a deep spiritual pain on top of the political anguish I was reeling under.

Who can understand the ways of God, when the grandson of a great religious leader like Hazrat Maulana Shah Abdul Aziz Mohaddis-e Delhi, who is still revered by all Hindustanis, is working as a lowly worker for a few pennies today!

The high and mighty of present day Hindustan can learn a life lesson from this. Perchance they will understand the transient nature of power and wealth.

Many shed copious tears on reading about the fate of the Alhambra palace of Spain and its residents, but no one weeps for the destruction and desolation of the residents of the Red Fort of Delhi.

The ancestral home of Mehmood Jaroobkash was in the Red Fort, a stone's throw from the *Khatib* office. That Red Fort where even the walls of the toilets and baths were encrusted with jewels, where slaves and attendants ran around to fulfil each wish and command. The man recently seen sweeping the newspaper office was once Prince Mehmood. His ancestors were the rulers of Hindustan. But today he came running to take and obey the orders of his master, the editor. Kings and nobles would stand in front of his ancestors with folded hands, just as he was standing before his employer today. Prince Mehmood may have forgotten but history remembers everything.

Mirza Mehmood may have learnt to bear his trials and tribulations with fortitude but my heart was agitated. How could I calm my heart?

Prince Mehmood stays in a hovel in which his lowliest slave wouldn't have lived. It has a mud wall, courtyard and roof. The mud walls are decorated with the ravages of the rains and time. The prince eats food which even his servants never had to eat. He eats dry chapatis with chutney and fills his stomach with boiled lentils. If he is not able to arrange for this, he tells his children to have patience and they go to sleep on an empty stomach.

Now he has neither brocade nor velvets, and this royal prince and his children now wear patched coarse cotton clothes. In winters they make do with torn blankets and old quilts.

Today, in December 1918, Congress and Muslim league are holding meetings in Delhi and the delegates who have come from outside sleep in cosy rooms tucked in warm blankets. While the new British rulers lie near a warm fireplace in the government house and chat about sundry things, Prince Mehmood and many other Timurid princes like him are struggling to survive poverty and the winter cold.

Merely 60 years ago the Red Fort was flourishing in this same Delhi. The ancestors of Prince Mehmood slept peacefully in gold and silver beds tucked in expensive shawls and blankets, without a worry in the world. They could not have imagined even in their worst dreams that their children would one day lead such a helpless and impoverished life. Had it occurred to them, I am sure they would have left a note for the luxury loving people of Delhi that they should always keep the vagaries of time in mind.

Today, if Prince Mehmood's children, remember their ancestors' 'glory' and ask their father for soft blankets, shawls and gold and silver beds, to eat pulao and korma in gold and silver plates, and want to be respectfully wished and addressed as Sahib-e Alam by everyone, what can poor Mehmood do, except weep silent tears at his fate?

The people of Delhi know that the princes of the Red Fort were attuned to the weather and would enjoy each with great alacrity. They would wear different dresses and eat different foods in each weather. They even distributed the same among the poor people of the city before using the items themselves. However, now Prince Mehmood's children are deprived of all these niceties. They wear and eat whatever is available, which is often insufficient. Spring and happiness have deserted their homes. They have forgotten that they are royal and are the descendants of the emperor of Hindustan and only know that they are the children of a man who goes to work at dawn and returns at dusk, earning ten rupees a month in return. These children have no idea that their ancestors once held durbars during the festival of Eid, distributing lakhs in charity to the poor. They know that they can't get new clothes or shoes on any Eid because they are expensive and their father can't afford it.

'The salary that my employer gave me has gone to the grocer for the flour yet I am still in debt. If God gives me more, I will buy you old shoes from the Chowk.'

The children would excitedly wait for those old clothes and shoes.

If their father fell prey to any seasonal disease, these innocent children would starve and raise their tiny hands in prayer and call out, 'Allah *Miyan*, please heal our father and make him well again.'

If the youngest child cried for food, the elder sister clutched him to her bosom and consoled him, 'Abbajan will get well soon and bring flour. Ammajan will cook it and you and I will eat hot *rotis*.'

'When will Abbajan get well? I am very hungry,' the child would ask.

'Don't fret so much. Abba will soon get well again and go to the market to buy flour for us.'

The child would go to his princess mother, already afflicted by fate, and say, 'Ammajan, give me a roti.'

The poor princess would embrace him tightly and say, 'Son, from where can I get a *roti* for you? May Allah save our bread earner. All my prayers and thoughts are concentrated on his recovery. *Miyan*, we are poor people and have no money for medicines, food or clothes. May God bless Hakim Ajmal Khan who arranged for the medicines. And may God keep our righteous neighbour, Mohammed Ali Karkhanadar, who is looking after all the sick people of this area. He had asked if we need food, but I was too embarrassed to accept his offer and acknowledge that there is no food in my house. How can we Timurids beg and accept charity? It is enough of an embarrassment for me that I have had to accept medicines for your father as charity.

'My son, you are the descendant of emperors and we don't beg or accept charity. When you grow up, you should also take up honest employment like your father and earn your food and not live on charity.'

The child would continue sobbing. 'Amma, I will not beg anyone else but at least I can ask you! Please give me something to eat.'

That helpless, indigent princess would look at the sky and cry out, 'O master, you are the one whom we worship, the one who provides for all. This poor child is crying with hunger; who can I turn to for my wants if not you? Please have pity on us and make my husband healthy again.'

By the Grace of God, Prince Mehmood would regain health and return to work. He earned enough to take care of the needs of his family.

If one were to study the trials and tribulations of this prince and his family, the contrast between their 'today' and 'yesterday' would tell them all they needed to know about the difference that time makes. If one wished to understand the highs and lows, honour and disgrace, independence and dependence of life with their own eyes without reading any deep philosophical books, they would just need to observe the life of the prince and his family.

O sweeper prince! Your present life and the life of your ancestors can serve as a warning to every ruler in this world, and to those seeking riches and power. Pride in possessions and rank disappear from the mind just as bubbles burst in the bright sun when one weighs the role of time.

And that is my aim in writing your story.

19

The Prophet's Descendant: Zakia Bayabani

Where is the smell of burnt hair coming from? Perhaps the neighbouring *amil*[81] is chanting an incantation. Since we have come to live next to a tantric this has become a constant nuisance.

Sometimes he burns clarified butter and sometimes gum-resin. The smells that emanate from his house are unbearable at times.

Zakia's mother, Naqia said, 'Yes, my dearest, he knows black magic and that requires such things to be burnt. I heard the day before that Nawab Zeenat Mahal has sent her special confidant to this tantric. Perhaps she needs some black magic performed against one of her enemies or maybe she wanted some incantations to increase her husband, Hazrat Sirajuddin Muhammad Bahadur Shah's love for her and keep him seduced. From the smell wafting across, I feel it is the first because hair is burnt to prepare hexes against enemies.'

Zakia replied, 'Bi, I have heard from Abbajan that hair is also burnt for incantations or spells that increase someone's love.'

'Anyway, whatever he is up to we are fed up with this nonsense. I don't know why your grandfather took up a house next to someone doing such irreligious and non-shariah acts,' replied Naqia.

---

81. An *amil* can be a worker, functionary, agent or necromancer. Here, he is a necromancer who practises black magic.

Just as Zakia was speaking, her father Hazrat Syed Nurul Huda entered the house. The seventy-year-old with a white beard was dressed in a white robe and turban. His fair face glowed with a spiritual light that comes from years of prayers and devotion to God.

Zakia got up to present her salutations.

'Babajan, you have come back after many days even though you had said you were only going to meet some officer in Gurgaon and would return after a day!' she said.

'Yes, my dear. I had to stay back as they didn't let me return. Have you learnt the forty hadith that I had taught you before leaving?" he asked.

'Yes, respected father, I have committed them to memory and even learnt their translation,' Zakia replied.

'However, I have some doubts related to the hadith: *Leave that which makes you doubt for that which does not make you doubt.*[82] I haven't been able to understand it clearly. How can we leave something which we have doubts about? It is beyond the capacity of any ordinary person to only adopt and believe those things which they have no doubts about. It is human nature to doubt everything. I don't know of anything which can be effectively proven to be hundred per cent without doubt!'

Syed Nurul Huda replied, 'My dear daughter, this hadith has been selected from three lakh hadiths and within it is a philosophy that every Muslim needs to follow in worldly and spiritual matters. There is another hadith which helps us at every step: *The reward of deeds depends upon the intentions and every person will get the reward according to what he has intended.*[83]

'The virtue or vice of our acts are determined on the basis of our intentions. If anyone performs a kind act with an evil intention, it will not be counted as a good act. In his register of deeds, God will note it down as an evil deed. And similarly, if some deed seems evil but has been performed with kindness, it will be counted as a good deed.

---

82. *Sunan an-Nasa'i* 5711
83. *Sahih al-Bukhari* 1

'Haven't you heard the story of the man who struck a peg in front of a mosque so that travellers could tie their horses to it while they offered their prayers? But no one tied their horses to the peg and instead stumbled against it in the dark and fell down. God had seen the man's intent and wrote it down under good deeds in his register.

'On the other hand, another man had put down a peg to trap travellers, make them fall down and suffer so that they were unable to pray. But instead of stumbling against the peg, they used it to tie their horses and went inside the mosque and prayed comfortably. This man's intent was evil so this act was recorded under evil deeds.

'So, everything is dependent on intent. In a few words, this hadith distinguishes between good and evil deeds till the Day of Resurrection. The case of the hadith that you asked about is also similar. Muslims have been instructed how to manage their worldly and spiritual affairs: stay away from doubt and adopt those actions which are clear of suspicion. There is no doubt that men of low intellect and less knowledge are not able to easily differentiate between which things to doubt and which ones to believe in. The hadith sharif are not meant to present difficulties in the path of Muslims but instead make their lives easier.

'You must have read the hadith: *The religion (of Islam) is easy.*[84] There is nothing in our religion which makes it difficult for us to follow it. This hadith makes it clear that Muslims should not live in a state of indecision but be absolutely sure of their actions and the direction they tread on.

'If one is in a state of indecision, he is always worried about whether what he is doing is good or evil. The Prophet, peace be upon him, did not want Muslims to live in a constant state of doubt and to stay away from anything they were unsure of.

'Let me explain with an example. One man says there is God, the second denies it, the third says he doesn't know whether there is a God and is plagued by doubts.

'Now, the first man is sure of God's existence so he is at peace, and the second one who denies it is also at peace. But the man who

---

84. Riyad as-Salihin 145

is indecisive is always uncomfortable and unhappy for he isn't sure whether to believe or not.

'This hadith means that in matters of religion, anything that appears against the Quran sharif and the teachings and hadith of the Prophet also appears contrary to intellect. But people say that this is not clear and try to shake your belief with their arguments. You should not be swayed. Stay firm on your path in the light and guidance of the Quran sharif and hadith.

'If your true friends and your own intellect have an opinion on some worldly matter and people have another opinion, you should stay with the first where there is no scope of doubt.'

'But this is exactly my question! How can a person of ordinary intellect differentiate between that which is clear and that to which some suspicion is attached? Zakia asked

Syed Nurul Huda replied, 'The job of fire is to burn. If someone says that fire doesn't burn then who will accept that? Similarly, God has given every person the capacity to understand what is good and what is bad for them.

'One man says, "I am a Muslim and I recite the Islamic creed, but my status is so elevated that if you don't revere me and give allegiance to me, then your belief in Allah and his messenger is also questionable. Submission to me is also compulsory for you."

'Now this statement is doubtful because in Islam a Muslim should acknowledge Allah as One and believe in Muhammad *pbuh*, as his messenger, and accept the Quran as his guidance. So, what is the need for him to accept some man, much like himself, as equal to Allah and his messenger and become his slave? We should not equate anyone with Allah or the Prophet. Allah, the Prophet and the Quran are enough for us. It is not necessary for us to believe in men who say that if we don't submit to them then our belief in Allah and the Prophet are in doubt too.'

Zakia replied, 'Then should we not obey those who guide us and show us the correct path?'

Syed Nurul Huda said, 'No this is not what I am saying. Allah has said in the Quran sharif that we must obey Allah, his messenger and those in authority. "Those in authority" refer to those people who show us the correct path. *O believers! Obey Allah and obey the Messenger and those in authority among you. Should you disagree on anything, then refer it to Allah and His Messenger, if you "truly" believe in Allah and the Last Day. This is the best and fairest resolution.*[85]

'I oppose those who insist that if we don't submit to them, our entire faith in Allah and his Messenger are in doubt and you can't be called a believer. This argument should be rejected.

'Obedience to Allah, the Prophet and the *ahl al- bait*, Household of the Prophet, is without doubt.'

Zakia asked, 'So if some imam or religious leader wants our submission to show us the right path in this world in the light of the Oneness of God, Quran and Hadith then that too would be obedience to a man and you should express doubt over that?'

Syed Nurul Huda replied, 'No. Obedience to such a man who guides you in the light of the Quran and the Prophet, is the same as obedience to Allah and the Messenger. If some religious leader asks you to stop reading the Quran and not to gain any independent knowledge of the religion and to only rely on what he says, he is not worthy of being obeyed. The first verse of the Quran sharif that was revealed instructed mankind to gain knowledge.[86] The Prophet has stated in hadith, *Seeking knowledge is an obligation upon every Muslim.*[87]

'Anyone who stops any Muslim from seeking knowledge or reading the Quran is only worthy of being rejected. The Prophet has ordered us to reject anything where we have any doubt.'

Zakia said, 'Now I have understood. The Prophet has given us such clear directions and may Allah give us the strength to walk on the right path.'

The Dream of 10 May 1857

On the morning of 10 May 1857, Syed Nurul Huda related a dream that he had seen at night to his wife Naqia and daughter

---

85. Surah An-Nisa - 4:59
86. Surah 96:1. Read, in the Name of your Lord Who created
87. Sunan Ibn Mājah 224

Zakia. He had seen a fearsome fire raining from the sky which was burning people and animals to death. He interpreted the dream as a warning for terrifying riots in the country.

Zakia asked, 'Why did you interpret the dream thus? It could also be related to some epidemic or natural calamity.'

Syed Nurul Huda replied, 'You do not have the knowledge that I do. God, in his mercy has given me the ability to foresee future events up to a hundred years. I can see my martyrdom, your trials and your piteous conditions with my own eyes. However, I can't protest, for whatever has been ordained by Him will happen.'

Hearing this, Zakia was terrified but as she was very well versed in the scriptures and other subjects, she replied, 'If you have already been told all this, why don't you pray for our safety?'

Syed Nurul Huda replied, 'I can't pray because I have already been told that the writing of eternity is ineradicable. There is no escape from the punishment of our deeds. There is no scope to change anything.

'O Zakia, I am the descendant of the eighth Shia imam, Imam Reza, and my lineage is pure till date. By the grace of God even my deeds are acceptable. My martyrdom is not a punishment for my personal misdeeds, but on the contrary, it is the *sunnat*, tradition, of my ancestors. Your mother and you should also keep in mind this tradition and bear all your troubles without complaints with fortitude. Our lives will serve the descendants of the Holy Prophet.'

Meaningless Words

After saying this, Syed sahib started chanting in a state of spiritual ecstasy [induced by remembrance of Allah] and started speaking.

'In the first year there will be blood, second year destruction—destruction of the crown, obstacles in the third year, descension and decline, epidemic and earthquake in the fourth. Thereafter, swings of fate—someone will ascend, someone will fall. Sixty years have passed since then and now, murder, disharmony and conflict—the sea has swallowed up the earth, the earth has swallowed the sun, brass and iron are making clanging sounds, tongues are silenced, a man worth tuppence is on the throne and the throne is in the hut—there is a red light of Badakshan in the earthen lamp—Zakia's children are suffering the pain of being slapped. Muslims are on the hills and trees are on the ground.'

After uttering these words, Syed sahib fell silent and started crying.

Zakia and Naqia were so frightened that they were speechless. They silently heard these wild utterances. Syed sahib got up and left.

Ghadar

Finally, the famous *ghadar* of 1857 started. The army of Meerut rebelled and came to Delhi and created havoc, leaving a trail of destruction behind them. Zakia and her father started living in a very humble house near the masjid of Tahavvur Khan.

Syed sahib avoided going out after that. Even when the British recaptured Delhi, the rebels ran away, Bahadur Shah ran away from the Qila and was arrested, the city was being looted and plundered, Syed sahib did not come out of his house. Finally, a regiment entered his house and arrested Syed sahib and looted everything. The officer of the regiment was an Englishman. He asked, 'Are you Syed Nurul Huda? And did you write letters to so and so officers of the army, that I have seen the assassination of Englishmen written on the *lauh-e mahfooz*, secret tablet on which the destiny of world is recorded?'

Syed sahib replied, 'Yes, I am the same Nurul Huda.'

The astonished officer said, 'You acknowledge your guilt?'

Syed sahib replied, 'I accept that I wrote the letters but not that I committed any crime.'

'Don't you think that it is a crime to write such made up stories and incite ignorant people to commit murder?' asked the officer.

Syed sahib just stayed silent and looking up towards the sky started laughing. His laughter angered the British officer and he hit Syed sahib on the lips with his bayonet. Syed sahib's jaw got cut and his beard was covered with blood.

Zakia shouted, 'O my poor Abbu!'

Syed sahib remained calm and showed no signs of agitation. He once again looked towards the sky and rubbed the blood on his face and chest. The officer indicated to his subordinate and that man swung such a blow with his sword that Syed sahib fell to the ground cut in two pieces.

The soldiers went out and did not trouble the women further. Zakia and Naqia started lamenting loudly. After a while they tried to make arrangements for the martyr's burial. There was no one in Delhi who could come to their help. The two women dug a grave in their courtyard and buried him in the same bloodied clothes.

Even though everything had been looted, some flour, lentils and firewood remained. For a few days they lived on the remnants but it soon ran out and they had to worry about their future.

At that time peace had been announced in the city and those who had fled the city were returning to resettle. Zakia, after taking advise from her mother, decided to write to the new ruler of Delhi, so that they could get some relief. Naqia said, 'You will be able to write the letter but who will deliver it?'

Zakia replied, 'I have heard that the *amil* sahib who lives next door, is a well-wisher of the new government and he did not run away in the *ghadar*. You give this letter to him.'

Naqia liked this idea and took the letter to the *amil*.

The *amil* was a young man, and from the state of his residence seemed very prosperous.

Naqia told him their circumstances from behind her burqa. The *amil* seemed very sympathetic but said, 'Don't expect mercy and sympathy from the ruler of Delhi. Syed sahib's name is listed as a leading rebel. If truth be told, he played a big role in inciting the army. If you agree, I can personally render some help.'

Naqia replied, 'We can't accept charity. If you give us some work, we will accept whatever you give in return for that.'

The *amil* said, 'Tell your daughter to make a list of all my books and gather all the scattered papers together. In return, I will send you two cooked meals daily and some money for your other expenses.'

Naqia conveyed the offer to Zakia who accepted it.

The *amil* showed them the room where his books were kept and Zakia and Naqia started working there from morning till evening.

A Letter in the Trash

Zakia was sorting out the papers when she saw a letter in the pile of trash. The subject of the letter was: '*Amil* sahib's *taveez* has reached and we are ready to do whatever is required of us, as per the directions. The *dhuni*, a fire lighted by a whimsical Hindu faqir over which he sits by way of penance, has come from Punjab. Whatever you have written about the venerable Syed Nurul Huda has been read by us. We will come shortly to meet him and honour him with gifts in keeping with his miraculous powers. We have some outer problems. Can you give us some solution to counter that? You had given us the address of some *amil* in Kashmir and we have decided to go there. The writer remains your devoted follower. N - N.'

Zakia was shocked to read this letter. After examining it minutely, she found out that this letter had been written by General Nicholson, who was camping on the ridge during the siege of Delhi. The word *taveez* referred to secret information sent by the *amil*—the reference to the *dhuni* from Punjab meant the army and magazine. These terms must have been created for the purpose of exchanging information. 'Outer problems' meant the batteries on the high ground and 'solution' referred to a way of breaching the walls of Delhi. 'Kashmir' referred to Kashmiri Darwaza which was stormed by the British forces and from where they entered Delhi. Giving a gift to Syed Nurul Huda meant murdering him.

Zakia understood that the letter 'N' meant General Nicholson. She knew that this same *amil* must have spied on her father. Her eyes filled up with tears. Darkness swelled up within her and she decided to take revenge for her father's death.

The next day, she went to the *amil*'s house with a knife in her hand, so that she could kill him while he was asleep. However, she found that the *amil* wasn't in his bedroom and returned home disappointed.

At home she found her mother's corpse drenched in blood. There was a letter kept near her head, which read, 'Zakia this is a revenge for your intentions. The consequence for becoming my opponent is that your mother has been murdered as she was an obstacle in the path of my love for you. Since you wanted to kill me, I pre-empted you and killed your mother. Now stay quiet for you have to leave Delhi.'

As soon as Zakia read the last sentence, she forgot her mother's tragic murder and wanted to scream and call her neighbours. Before she could open her mouth, someone came from behind and caught her, covering her mouth.

Ambala

Zakia was gagged and blindfolded and after a while she fainted. When she regained consciousness, she found herself in a strange house with the *amil* sitting in front of her.

He told her, 'You are in Ambala as I have come to seek shelter with the British. I hope you have forgotten your intention of seeking revenge for your father's death?'

Zakia retorted, 'Have some shame. I am of Syed descent, and you are a *na-mahram*, stranger with whom purdah is obligatory.'

The *amil* said, 'Don't worry about that. I will just get the nikah solemnised and will become *mahram*, legal, for you.'

Zakia hid her face with her hands and started thinking of her helpless condition.

Blood

As soon as she hid her face, she heard a loud sound. A man cursing loudly, hit the *amil* on the head. When she uncovered her face, she found that the *amil*'s servant had killed him by delivering a blow on the *amil*'s head with a stick.

He told Zakia to escape quickly, 'I have come to rescue you.'

Zakia got up and ran with him. There was a *rath* waiting outside and both of them got into it and drove away.

Karnal

The servant brought Zakia to Karnal, where he lived. He took Zakia to his house and left her with his mother. He said, 'Bibi, I heard you say that you are of Syed descent. I thought it was better to kill the *amil* who harboured evil intentions towards you. Now, please pray that I am not arrested.' He was just saying all this when he heard some policemen calling out to him. The servant said, 'Lo! My death has arrived. Amma, Khuda Hafiz. Take care of this woman. I am going to escape. If I live, I will return. Otherwise, this is my last *salam* to you.'

Saying this, he ran away from another door. The police called out thrice and when they didn't get an answer, they entered the house. They found footsteps leading out of the other doorway and followed them. However, they could not find the *amil*'s murderer.

Finally, the government sent orders for the confiscation of the servant's house and auctioned everything in it. The servant's mother went to live with some relative. She took Zakia with her. However, the relative refused to let them stay there and said, 'You are connected to someone who is a criminal in the eyes of law. I can't let you stay here.'

The servant's mother tried to find refuge in the houses of all her relatives and son's friends but all of them refused.

Out of sheer desperation the old woman told Zakia, 'Let us go to a mosque. That is God's house and we should find shelter there.'

However, the *mullah*[88] in the mosque refused to let them in. 'Women aren't allowed inside a mosque,' he said.

Zakia said, 'We are helpless orphans who have no refuge in this world. Thus, we came to seek shelter in God's house. Don't refuse to let us come in as we have no other place left to go to. Where else can we go for no one is letting us enter their house. Have some fear of God and don't turn away his desperate creatures from his house.'

---

88. A *mullah* is different from a *maulvi*. He was a scholar of the religion or is very well versed in it. He would just know enough to lead the prayers.

The *mullah* laughed and said, 'This is a place to recite prayers not an inn where you can live. It will be better for you to go away peacefully or else I will drag you out of here by your hair!'

The old woman started crying and said, 'This girl is of Syed descent. Don't disrespect her with such insulting words.'

The *mullah* said, 'I have seen many such women of Syed descent. Just go away from here and stop making excuses.' He then pushed them away.

The old woman fell down in front of the mosque. She lost her remaining two teeth in the fall and fainted. Zakia supported her up and wiped the blood from her face with her dupatta and said, 'Amma, don't worry. Please get up. God will help us.'

The old woman said in a feeble voice, 'Yes, my daughter, God is our only help. I have been badly hurt on my chest and am finding it difficult to breathe. I was already sick and on top of that my son's separation, the confiscation of the house, the attitude of my relatives and the *mullah* and now this fall! I don't think there is any hope for me. My heart has been wounded. I am going to die.'

The old woman started vomiting blood which showed that her lungs had been injured in the fall. She fainted and Zakia was distressed.

The old lady regained consciousness in a bit and said, 'O *Mullah*, you have unjustly taken my life. I came here with this orphan *saidani*. Now I am dying. I will go to my Prophet pbuh, and put my head on the feet of his daughter, Bibi Fatima. I will tell her that I have sacrificed my young son for one of your daughters and now gave up my life for her. Bibi Fatima will embrace me and the Prophet will ask Hazrat Ali to give a sip of water from the holy Kausar.[89] Aah, I go.'

She vomited again and with a hiccup left this world.

It was a strange scene. Zakia was cradling the old lady's corpse at the door of the mosque and looking around for some sympathizer. There was no one there; not even a traveller going past who could help. The *mullah* had closed the door of the mosque.

---

89. The river of milk and nectar, called *Kausar*, is fabled to flow in Paradise.

Finally, Zakia looked up towards the sky in desperation and called out, 'O Allah I am a descendant of your beloved Prophet *pbuh*. Please listen to my pleas.'

A faqir passing by saw this scene and went and called the people from the neighbouring locality. They asked Zakia what had happened.

Zakia did not complain about the *mullah*'s behaviour and just asked the people to arrange for the old lady's burial.

Arrangements were made and Zakia accompanied the funeral bier till the graveyard.

After the burial she saw that the faqir who had come to the mosque lived in a hut that was very old. Zakia went up to him and said, 'Baba, give me some place to live.'

The faqir replied, 'My daughter, this is your house. You are welcome to live here.'

The faqir would go begging every day and bring back food for both of them.

Zakia Goes Begging

The faqir fell sick after a few days and asked Zakia, 'My daughter, now you will have to go to the city and beg for food for us.'

Initially Zakia thought to herself, 'I am a *saidani* and I can't beg.' However, she also realized that she had been living on the scraps that the faqir got from begging so why should she hesitate now?

Desperation makes a person do anything!

So, she wore her burqa, took the beggar's pouch in her hand and went to beg in the city. When she reached the first *mohalla* she called out, 'This world is the flower of a cactus. If someone is enamoured of the world, they are making a grievous error. Why are you filled with pride over a life that is limited to a few breaths? Always keep in mind that death is ever-present. Why do you sleep a heedless sleep and lose valuable time? Gear up, get ready to give up worldly pursuits and involve yourselves in spiritual pursuits that will improve your afterlife. A morsel of bread dissolves once added to the curry. Similarly, the heart once soaked in greed, becomes numb. A narcissistic piece of coal also singes but the ember ultimately becomes ash. *And in heaven is your provision, and that you are promised* (Quran 51:22).

'I supplicate with reference to this verse of the Holy Quran, for what can a mere mortal give me? The giver is Allah, the One who is blessed with might and glory.'

All those who heard her call were moved by it. All the learned people of the locality gathered around her and filled her pouch with food.

One said, 'Bibi, go to that house in front. An assembly has been arranged on the occasion of Muharram. After the sermon has been delivered, food will be distributed among the destitute.'

Zakia went to the assembly where thousands were present, and found that the *mujtahid*, a Shia religious scholar, delivering the sermon was extolling the praises of the Prophet and his family.

Finally, the *mujtahid* said, 'Alas! If only we were present in the battlefields of Karbala and could sacrifice our lives and possessions on Imam Hussain, or that we could sacrifice our lives on the trials and tribulations faced by the later imams. We are slaves of the family of Mohammad and are ready to ransom our lives for them. Our whole life is spent under their feet. Today this pomp and show, all this splendour is for the sake of the descendants of the Prophet. Today, many such assemblies must be taking place in the memory of the Prophet's descendants.'[90]

On hearing this, Zakia called out in a loud voice, 'I have something to say, please listen to me.'

The congregation tried to silence her asking her not to insult the *mujtahid*, 'Let the respected scholar finish what he is saying.'

---

90. Prophet Muhammad had only one surviving daughter, named Fatima. She was also called Syeda. She was married to Ali ibn Abi Talib, the fourth of the rightly guided caliphs. Hazrat Ali, as he is also called, was considered to be the first of the infallible imams or leaders of the Shia sect of Muslims. Their descendants are called *saiyeds* (male) or *saidani* (female). The famous battle of Karbala where their son Imam Hussain was martyred along with his friends and male members is commemorated in the Islamic month of Muharram, every year by holding assemblies in his name. Even though Islam has established a classless society the *saiyeds* as descendants of the Prophet hold a high position and are generally respected.

The *mujtahid* was also frowning. He said, 'What a rude woman!'

Zakia said, 'Don't be angry. You have delivered your sermon now listen to the person on whose plight you are heaving these sighs. I am a descendant of the eighth imam[91], Imam Raza, even though I am a beggar who has had to face the adversities of this world and have been rendered homeless and penniless. I am now Zakia Bayabani, Zakia of the Wilderness.'

The pain and anguish in Zakia's voice attracted everyone's attention and everyone including the *mujtahid* stared at her. Finding everyone's attention on her, Zakia started speaking.

'Let the *Mujtahid* sahib, and all the gathered crowd know that Imam Husain and his descendants are still facing the afflictions of Karbala. The flowers of Husain's gardens are withering in the heat of cruelty and oppression. In every lane, you will find the descendants of Bibi Fatima being inflicted with pain and sorrow. Even today the *syed*s are bearing the tyranny of modern day Yezids.[92] What use are your false sighs of sympathy? Had you been present in the battlefield of Karbala you would have been as heedless of the family of the Prophet as you are today. Had you had been present in the time of the infallible imams, you would have been as selfish and self-centred as you are today, offering lip service. None amongst you would have gone to their help.

'O *Mujtahid* sahib, you all earn fame and name in our name, rule over the hearts of the true lovers of the family of the Prophet. But none of you have any sympathy for this daughter of Bibi Fatima.

---

91. The Shias consider twelve imams, starting with Ali who was the son-in-law and cousin of the Prophet and their descendants as the spiritual and political successors of the Prophet.

92. Yezid was the second caliph of the Umayyad dynasty. Imam Hussain, the third Shia imam, had refused to take an oath of allegiance to him, rejecting his appointment as a caliph on the grounds that he was morally and spiritually unfit for the post. Imam Hussain had left for Iraq from Medina to avoid a confrontation, which would result in bloodshed. However, Yezid's forces intercepted him in the plains of Karbala in Iraq. A battle ensued between the army of Yezid and the motley crew of 72 friends and relatives who had accompanied Imam Hussain on the journey. All male members were martyred, leaving an ailing son, Zain al-Abidin, who became the fourth Shia Imam, and the widowed women and orphaned children.

Your purpose in organizing these assemblies isn't to serve the family of the Prophet but to use their name for your personal reputation and wealth. These sweets and food aren't being distributed for the love of us. This reeks of ostentation and superficiality and your greed to attain name and fame at our cost. The sincere believers give you their treasures and assets for the love of us and you spend them for your own selfish purposes to buy expensive house, clothes and keep servants so that you can live a life of luxury. You don't spend a single penny for the descendants of the Prophet. Tell me, what share of the crores being spent in all the assemblies being held all over the world to commemorate the sacrifices of Imam Hussain and the Prophet's family is given to the living family of the Prophet? How many of them are being saved from penury and starvation? How much is being spent on the education and upbringings of the *ahl al-bait*, the Prophet's family? Have you ever bothered to find out how poor helpless *saidani*s are trying to eke out a respectable living?

'Why are you silent? Do you have an answer? What can you say? You are ashamed and my plain speaking has embarrassed you.'

Mujtahid sahib replied, 'Seek forgiveness and give a message to all those learned men and religious scholars who claim to love the Prophet's descendants and claim to be leaders of those who are sincerely devoted to the *ahl al-bait*. On the day of Resurrection, the Prophet will ask them for an account of their false promises. Amir al-Momineen Hazrat Ali and Bibi Syeda Mazlooma Bibi Fatima will also ask them, "Were you only offering lip service or did you do anything to alleviate the trouble of my family?"'

The gathered assembly was shocked into silence after hearing Zakia and had nothing left to say.

Zakia left quietly and went back to the graveyard.

After a few days, she married a sweet-tempered man. He was a Syed and was a cloth trader and on Zakia's insistence made a house for them inside the graveyard. Zakia spent her whole life in this house.

Every Friday Zakia would deliver a sermon on the transient nature of life and thousands would gather to hear her homilies.

She became famous as Zakia Bayabani. She is still known all over the world by that name.[93]

One should learn from the things that Zakia had told the *mujtahid*. His Highness Sir Aga Khan, the head of the Bohra community Tahir Saifuddin sahib, and all the religious leaders, sheikhs who invoke the name of Bani Fatima[94] and hold religious assemblies and become the leaders of the community but have no sympathy for the descendants of the Prophet, except to make their own groups and sects. They take countless amount of money in the name of the Prophet's descendants and live a grand life of luxury. I want to wake them up and shake them out of their apathy just as I have done it two years ago in my book *Yazid nama* where I had named some people too. However, no one has paid any heed to my words in these intervening two years.

---

93. The 1934 and 1942 edition stop at this line. The passage that follows is given in the 2008 edition and must have been added by Khwaja Hasan Nizami at a later date.
94. Though Bani Fatima is used to refer to the Fatamids, a Shia Caliphate established in 10th century in parts of North Africa, here Zakia means the descendants of Bibi Fatima known as syeds and saidanis.

20

Two Princes in the Jailhouse

Mirza Tegh Jamal is now around eighty years old. He was a strapping nineteen-year-old man in the *ghadar* of 1857. He remembers everything that happened before the *ghadar* and describes the events as if they happened yesterday!

Mirza Tegh Jamal is the son of Mirza Fakhru, the second heir apparent. The first heir apparent of Emperor Bahadur Shah was his eldest son, Mirza Dara Bakht. After Mirza Dara's death, Mirza Fakhru was appointed as the heir apparent.

Mirza Fakhru was a very religious and pious prince. Had the monarchy of Delhi remained, he would have gone down as an excellent and upright emperor.

However, even the most righteous become wayward and are led astray in their youth. Mirza Fakhru was the son and heir of the reigning emperor of Hindustan who had no one or anything to fear, when playing hide and seek with pleasures of youth. At that time the Lal Qila was infamous for the wayward ways of its princes and their predilection for courtesans.

So, if Mirza Fakhru got swept away by the passions of youth and committed a mistake it was not considered anything extraordinary or out of the way.

Mirza Tegh Jamal was the result of this very interesting first and secret mistake. His mother did not bear any other children after him.

The other offsprings of Mirza Fakhru, such as Mirza Farkhanda Jamal, were from his legally wedded wives. That is why Mirza Farkhanda was awarded a pension of one hundred and fifty rupees by the British, but Tegh Jamal did not even get five rupees.

Tegh Jamal had a cheerful and pleasant personality. He felt no sorrow at not getting a pension or not being acknowledged as a prince. He would relate the tale of his parents' love affair with so much enthusiasm and enjoyment as if he was absolutely unconnected to it. Even though, he was a living example of the exaggerated and infamous, secret love stories that flourished in the Lal Qila.

Tegh Jamal says, 'Ammajan was sixteen years old and Abbajan was a little older than thirteen when their romance started.'

When he was asked how a thirteen-year-old boy could have a romantic liaison with a sixteen-year-old girl he would reply with a straight face, 'Just as an eighty-year-old man falls in love and professes his passion for a sixteen-year-old young girl!

'We Mughals matured very fast. Mughal girls would often attain puberty at the age of ten or eleven and boys would reach puberty at the age of twelve or thirteen and start thinking of and indulging in romance and love making. I found more passion in myself at the age of twelve than I do in eighteen-year-olds today.'

Tegh Jamal continued, 'Ammajan was the daughter of a *kahar*, porter. My grandmother was considered one of the most attractive *kaharan*, female porter, in the Lal Qila. She was a favourite of Akbar Shah II, who showered his favours on her. But my grandmother's charms were not a patch on mother's beauty and coquettish airs.

'Though Ammajan was a royal employee she mostly lived in the Khanum ka Bazaar with my maternal grandfather and grandmother. All the *kahars* of my maternal family lived here.

One day Abbajan went with the *darogha* of the *doerhi*, entrance to the mahal, to Khanum ka Bazar to get his bow repaired. Here he saw Ammajan and was instantly infatuated by her. After coming home, he went into a depression and started crying. Everyone asked him what the matter was but he kept weeping. My Dadi Amma said, "Has someone said anything to you? Has anyone gone against your wishes? Please tell me. I will find a solution."

'However, he was in the throes of passion and would only keep weeping silently.

'Finally, the true reason was found out and everyone in the mahal started talking of it and teasing the young boy. The begums started teasing Abbajan too, and the boys of his age were merciless in taunting him. When Nani Amma found out, she brought my Ammajan to the mahal and handed her over to Dadi Amma and got her name registered as one of the latter's employees.

'However, despite all this Abbajan was very shy and embarrassed to talk to Ammajan. If Ammajan saw him anywhere alone, she would hold his hand and ask, "Sahib-e Alam why are you so sad?"

'Abbajan would pull his hand and run away without speaking to her. This is what was apparent but no one knows what was happening and how Mirza Tegh Jamal was born!'

Mirza Tegh Jamal states that when he was born his mother was seventeen years old and father was fourteen and a half.

'Dadi Amma was very keen that after her grandson had been born to the *kaharan*, she should live in the palace like a begum. But Nani Amma did not accept it. Ammajan went back to Khanum ka Bazar with me and lived there.'

Mirza Tegh Jamal was six years old when he was sent to the Lal Qila to live with his father.

'Bhai, I am a *kahar* from my maternal side and an emperor from my father's side,' he would say. 'As a porter we bore the burden of humans on our back and as emperors we had to shoulder the responsibilities of humans. No one can compare their lives with us for we are destined to shoulder the responsibilities of God's creation in either case.'

Twenty Years After the *Ghadar*

Mirza Tegh Jamal says, 'During the days of the *ghadar*, I escaped from Delhi with my mother and came to Shahjahanpur[95], where my maternal family lived. I had left the company of my royal

---

95. Shahjahanpur is a city in present day Uttar Pradesh.

family when I saw the way they were being persecuted and went to my mother. The life of Mughal princes wasn't worth twopence in those days. It seemed prudent to me to live with my *kahar* family and be known as one of them. Ammajan had quite a lot of wealth that we could live comfortably. I opened a sweet shop in Shahjahanpur and twenty years were spent living well.'

He continued, 'One day a Pathan abused me saying that the sweets were not up to the mark. I had Mughal blood running in my veins. How could I bear to hear abuse? I picked up an iron rod lying nearby and hit the Pathan with so much force that he fell to the ground and died within five minutes, after writhing in agony. I was caught and after fighting the case for long, I was sentenced to 14 years' imprisonment.'

Bareilly's Jailhouse

Mirza Tegh Jamal continued his story:

'The first day that I stepped into the jail in Bareilly I was not at all agitated or upset at being imprisoned. My temperament was such that from my birth I was very cheerful and contented and never let any sorrows affect me. I remained happy even in jail. When Ammajan came to meet me in jail, she started weeping on seeing me there. I laughed and said, "Oh Ammajan, why are you crying? I have left enough sweets in the shop that you can spend many months eating them."

'Ammajan said angrily, "You are always clowning. Who else do I have to take care of me for fourteen years? I have spent twenty years in this strange land because of you, otherwise this village doesn't compare to Delhi."

'I replied, "When Abbajan's entire family has been ruined and huge mansions have been reduced to dust, what are fourteen years? They will vanish in the blink of an eyelid. Just take care of my wife and don't hurt her with your ill-tempered ways. You have the temperament of a queen while she is just a poor *kaharan*. Please don't hurt her with your royal temper."

Ammajan started laughing and went away saying, "I don't know how you have become so shameless and impudent. Anyway, I leave you in the care of God."

'When I was given the jail clothes to wear, I jokingly said, let these under drawers be! I prefer my pyjamas to them. The *warder*, armed guard, was very angry when he heard this and hit me hard with his club. He said, "This is not your Nani Amma's house that you are so amused."

'Even after bearing the blows of his club, I laughed and said, "Bhai Nani Amma's house was in Khanum ka Bazar and that has been demolished along with the entire *mohalla*. Dadi Amma's house was the Lal Qila which is now occupied by the British. I have come to this jail thinking that this is my *sasural*, in-law's house. I have heard that sons-in-laws are hit by shoes[96] but I have never heard of anyone being struck by clubs.

'The *warder* was so angry that he called a few other guards and they hit me so badly that I fainted. When I regained consciousness, I was lying in a cell with the *warder* standing in front of me.

'I said, now that you have completed the ceremony of welcoming me to my *sasural*, please call your sister so that she can bring food for me and can put a paste of *haldi-chuna*[97] on my wounds.

'The warder started laughing spontaneously. "Are you a human or a stone? Nothing seems to affect you. *Miyan*, this is a jailhouse and it is difficult to stay cheerful. You have to spend fourteen years here. If you conform and obey the rules, it will be easy for you. Otherwise, you will die in fourteen days from the beatings by the guards."

'I said, "Even after death one has to go into the prison of the grave but I feel very angry at the corpse. Why does he wear a shroud and go quietly into his grave? I will not stay silent after death and I will ensure that all those around me also don't stay silent. If you doubt me, you can die just now and check it out. Or, if you prefer, I can kill you."

---

96. Some of the fun ceremonies after the wedding in the in-laws' house which include horse-play.
97. Paste of turmeric and lime which heals internal wounds.

'The warder thought that I was a lunatic and went away laughing.

After a while they took me to the mill-house where two people grind wheat on a mill-stone. My partner there was an old man, who must have been just imprisoned and brought to jail, for he was weeping uncontrollably. I bent double and presented a *farshi salam*, a *kornish* for non-royals. and said, "Nana Abba, why are you weeping? Your devoted servant is a cross-breed: half a Timurid prince and the other half a *kahar*. Now that I will grind the mill-stone with you, a third aspect will be added to my personality."

'The old man didn't pay any attention to my words. He was so disconsolate and sad that eventually I got affected by it too and I told him, "You sit down I will grind the wheat for both of us, alone."

'He didn't reply to that either and kept weeping. The warder came and caught his white beard and gave him a few slaps. The poor man looked at the sky despairingly and started grinding the wheat. I was so affected by his grief that I forgot all my mischief and quietly ground the wheat with him. This state of affairs continued for many days. I would try to speak to him but he would keep weeping and ignore me. After eight days he finally opened up to me and told me his story.'

The Story of Shah Alam's Great Grandson

'I am the son of Mirza Jahangir, who was the son of the emperor of Delhi, Akbar Shah II. He was the brother of Bahadur Shah. When my father Mirza Jahangir shot at Seton sahib he was exiled to Allahabad as punishment and kept in house arrest.[98] He married my mother in Allahabad. She was the daughter of the officer in charge of the guards there.

'From the time of the wedding till my birth, my father gave so much wealth to my Nana and my mother that it was enough to keep seven generations in luxury. My Dadi would regularly send gems and gold coins for my father from Delhi. They had immense wealth.

---

98. Mirza Jahangir, the favourite son of Akbar Shah Alam II, took a potshot at the British resident, Sir Archibald Seton in the Red Fort and was exiled to the Allahabad Fort. He continued his dissolute ways there and died of alcoholism in 1821.

'After my father's death I was brought up under my Nana's aegis. I was brought up with so much coddling and love that I doubt any other child in the world received such a pampered upbringing.

'When I grew up, I was given the best of education available. After finishing my education, I opened a clothes shop. I would spend my day in the shop and nights in devotion of God. I have four children and my old mother is still alive.

'One day a *thanedar*, police inspector, came to buy some clothes in my shop. As was my custom I gave him a fixed price. He tried to bargain but I replied, "*Janab*, I have a fixed price in my shop and no false words are uttered in my shop."

'He got very angry on hearing my words and said, "You pretend to be very honest! I have sent many thugs like you to the jail."

I said, "*Thanedar*, please be careful in your choice of words. This is not how gentlemen speak."

'He was infuriated on hearing this and slapped my cheek hard. After all, I also had Mughal blood running in my veins and I slapped him back twice in return. The soldiers caught me and took me to the police station. The *thanedar* locked me up and sent his soldiers to search my house. They planted some stolen clothes in my house and filed a case of theft against me.

'I kept protesting my innocence and related the true events but my pleas fell on deaf ears. I was sentenced to six months of imprisonment.

'My old mother and wife sold all our possessions to fight my case. They were reduced to penury but it was of no avail. I was sent to prison. I am distraught because my mother had come to meet me when I was in the police station jail. She couldn't bear to see me in this state and fell down in shock, shrieking. Unable to bear this sorrow she left this world.

'My twelve-year-old son had accompanied her. He was shaken up and started crying, "Abbajan, Dadijan has died."

'I wanted to see my mother and touch her but the tyrant *darogha* beat me up and brought me here. My mother's corpse was left in the *thana*. As I was being taken away, I heard my son say, "Abbajan where should we go? Now these constables will beat us too. How will I take Dadijan home? Abbaji, Abbaji please don't go."

'I am dying by inches in this sorrow. I don't know what state my wife and children are in and how that cruel *thanedar* has treated them.

Mirza Tegh Jamal let out an involuntary guffaw. 'This world is a strange place. Both of us are in the same boat and are related to each other by blood. You are drowning in the depth of sorrow while I am buoyed up by my optimism and living in the sky of happiness," he said.

'*Waah waah*! God has created one kind of man. They eat the same food, wear the same clothes, they sleep and wake up the same but they were given such different temperaments. One is engulfed by cruelty and oppression and the other is the oppressor. One wallows in sorrow the other is buoyed up by happiness.

'Bhai sahib, both you and I will live out the term of our imprisonment. You will find this life unbearable and difficult to live, while I will go through the jail term cheerfully without thinking about it. I will remain optimistic and happy till I die.'

21

The Green-clad Woman's War

The old men of Delhi who were in their youth during the *ghadar* of 1857 relate the story of an old Muslim woman.[99] This was the time when the British had opened a front on the ridge and were bombarding the city from the direction of Kashmiri Darwaza. She would come every day into the city bazars and would call out in a very loud voice, 'Come, Come, God has invited you to paradise.'

The people of the city would gather around her on hearing her rallying cry and she would take them with her to the Kashmiri Darwaza. There, they would attack the British. She would exhort the city residents to fight from morn to night.

Some eyewitnesses say that this woman was amazingly courageous. She had no fear of death and would advance amongst the hail of bullets like any brave soldier. Sometimes she would be

99. In *Dastan-e-Ghadar*, Zahir Dehlvi relates this story: 'There was one old woman who would wear a headband and tie a dupatta around her waist and be right in front during the fight, instigating the soldiers: "Come on, sons, let's go for Jihad!" We didn't know who she was. She would gather people from the market every day and take them to fight. Though she led them, she always returned safe and sound, while hundreds were slain because of her.

When the army entered the city, no one could find her. She simply disappeared.' Zahir Dehlvi, *Dastan-e-Ghadar*, translated by Rana Safvi, (Penguin Random House, 2017).

on foot and sometimes mounted on a horse. She would be carrying a sword, a gun and a flag. She was an expert at using the gun. One of the men who had accompanied her to the ridge said that she was an expert at swordplay too. She often used her sword to fight one on one with the enemy forces.

The city residents were all enthused by seeing her bravery and courage and would accompany her in the attacks on the British forces. However, most of the residents were untrained in the art of war and would often have to retreat.

When she saw them turning around, the woman would urge them to stay back and fight. When she found that she was unlikely to succeed on her own, she would go back too. However, no one knew where she disappeared every evening after returning and from where she emerged the next morning.

One day, full of enthusiasm, using her sword and gun, she fought her way up to the ridge. There, she was wounded and fell off her horse. The British forces arrested her and no one knew what happened to her after that. [100]

The Martyrdom of a British Officer During the *Ghadar*

The government of the district of Delhi published some letters written in English by British officers during the siege of Delhi. Among those letters, there was one letter by W.R. Hodson sahib on 29th July, 1857 from the Delhi camp to Colonel Forsyth,

---

100. In *Twelve Years of a Soldier's Life in India: Being extracts from the letters of the late Major W. S. R. Hodson* published in 1859, by John Parker and Son, West Strand, London and edited by his brother Rev Goerge H. Hodson, there is a reference to this lady where Hodson writes:

"I have sent one of our few prisoners up to Forsyth at Umbala, whom we ironically call the "Maid of Delhi," though her age and character are questionable, and her ugliness undoubted. She actually came out on horseback, and fought against us like a fiend. The General at first released her, but knowing how mischievous she would be among those superstitious Mohammedans, I persuaded him to let her be recaptured, and made over for safe custody." The letter to Forsyth is not given in this book and I could not access it online.

Deputy Commissioner of Ambala.[101] This letter threw light on that old Muslim lady.

The letter said,

"My dear Forsyth,

I am sending one old Muslim woman to you. She is a strange one. She would dress in green clothes and enthuse the city residents into rebellion. She would arm herself and lead them into skirmishes. The soldiers who came in contact with her say that she attacked many a times with great courage and masculine valour. She used her weapons with great alacrity and her strength equalled that of five men.

The day she was arrested she had mounted a horse and was leading the city residents in a military fashion. She had a gun which she used to target and the soldiers say that she killed many among them with her sword and gun. However, as was expected, her companions ran away and she was wounded and arrested.

She was presented before the general who ordered her release on the grounds of her gender. However, I stopped him and said that if she was released, she would go into the city and claim spiritual and esoteric powers, and people of weak faith would think that there was some kind of divine intervention involved in her release. It is possible that like the famous Frenchwoman,[102] mentioned in the history of the French revolution, she may become a thorn in our flesh.

The general accepted my advice and gave orders for this woman to be jailed. I am sending her to you and hope that you will make suitable arrangements for her incarceration because this witch is a very dangerous woman.

—Hodson"

The Truth of the Green-clad Woman

Based on the stories told by the Delhi residents and the letter of the government officer, I tried to find out the truth about this

---

101. Deputy commissioner of Ambala. I have translated it from Urdu so some words in the letter may vary from the original.

102. A reference to Joan of Arc

green-clad woman. However, I could not find even one credible source.

Those who knew this woman could only narrate the stories of how she would come and rally the people of Delhi and enthuse them to fight. None of them knew from where she came and where she went.

Nevertheless, I heard one incident which seemed similar and it is possible that it features the same woman.

A man from the princely state of Tonk, narrated that his father was the disciple of Haji Lal Mohammed sahib Chishti Nizami. Haji sahib was the *khalifa*, successor, of Hazrat Maulana Fakhruddin Chishti Nizami Dehlvi. His shrine could be seen near the western gate of Hazrat Khwaja Nizamuddin Auliya in a marble enclosure. The man from Tonk said, 'My father took the oath of allegiance with Haji sahib in Ajmer Sharif. When he took that oath one *mazjoob*[103] woman was present. She was saying, "Please pray for my martyrdom."

Even though she spoke as one totally in control, her actions and appearance seemed like one who had lost her senses.

For a long time, Haji sahib didn't reply. Eventually he said enthusiastically, "You should strive for *jihad-ul nafs*, the internal struggle against the base self, for that is the highest struggle."

The woman said, "So will my *nafs*, base self, kill me? When I attain martyrdom, I will kill my *nafs* and will accept the martyrdom of the slaves of *nafs*."

Haji sahib smiled. He replied after a short silence, "The leaves of henna are green but hide a red interior. Go and be green and become red."

This metaphor was beyond our understanding but that woman fell on the Haji sahib's feet and after kissing them, left.

From her expression it was clear that she had understood Haji sahib's meaning and had got what she wanted.

After a few days I saw that woman in the dargah of Qutub sahib, Hazrat Qutbuddin Bakhtiyar Kaki. She was sitting in deep contemplation at the shrine of Hazrat Maulana Fakhruddin. When

---

103. One who is wholly absorbed in divine meditation to the exclusion of all else.

she was done, I asked her, "Are you the same woman that I saw in Ajmer Sharif?"

'She replied, "Yes, I am the same woman and I am your *pir-behen*, someone who has taken an oath of allegiance to the same spiritual master.

I said, "Oh! You have also taken an oath of allegiance with Haji sahib?"

She replied, "Yes, I am his slave."

I asked her, "Where is your house and since when did you become a mendicant?"

She narrated her story to me.

"My grandfather was a chief in Ahmad Shah Abdali's army. He was present in the battle of Panipat against the Marathas and was martyred there. My father was also in Ahmed Shah's army but he was very young at that time. He spent some time with his widowed mother in Lahore and then went with her to Bhawalpur state. There he took up a lowly employment to make ends meet and also got married. They had two sons but both of them died. I was born after that and spent my initial years in Bhawalpur. Thereafter, I came with my parents to Jaipur where my father had found employment. He died there and I got married to a Muslim chief in Raja sahib's employ."

The Orders of the Saint of Hindustan

"My husband was very sick and there was no hope left and I was sitting by his bed, praying when involuntarily the name of Hind al-Vali[104] Khwaja Moinuddin Chishti came to my lips. I prayed, O God, please restore my husband's health for the saint's sake. I went to sleep while praying and dreamt that there everything around me was aflame. People were pouring water to douse the flames but then the water burst forth as fire from the water containers. I was very frightened by this spectacle and saw an

---

104. A title of Khwaja Moinuddin Chishti. It means the Saint of Hindustan.

old gentleman standing there. He said, 'O woman sacrifice your head, only then will this fire be extinguished.'

I replied, 'Why should I sacrifice my head?'

The old gentleman asked, 'Don't you know how to attain martyrdom?' Saying so, he gave me a green chador and asked me to wear it. As soon as I wore it, I flew away in the breeze. The higher I flew the more sounds I heard from everywhere, 'She is a martyr, she is a martyr.' As soon as I heard this my eyes opened. I found that my husband was in a swoon. He left this world in that state.

My husband's death affected me deeply. I became crazed with grief. I went to Ajmer Sharif and started living there. I was blessed to meet Hazrat Haji sahib there and then had the honour of taking an oath of allegiance with him.

Now, I was all alone in this world for I had lost my parents and husband and since then I am convinced that Hind al-Vali Khwaja Moinuddin Chishti has ordered me to sacrifice my life and it was him that I saw in my dream. Now I have come for pilgrimage to the holy shrines of Delhi. I have spent most of my time at the shrine of Dada-pir Maulana Fakhr.

Yesterday, Dada-pir had visited me in my dream and said, 'You are the Sabzposh Shaheed, green-clad martyr.'"

The gentleman from Tonk said that after hearing this strange story he returned to his city.

A few days later the *ghadar* started in Delhi and that is what led me to deduce that this story was about the same green-clad woman who led the residents and she acted thus in a state of spiritual frenzy.

Secrets of the Universe

If she was indeed the same woman who fought in the *ghadar* and exhorted others to join her, it will be remembered in history as an incredible event. However, I feel that the tale narrated by the gentleman from Tonk did not bear too much similarity to the green-clad woman of the *ghadar*. She was indeed the granddaughter and daughter of soldiers but there is no information on how and where she learnt how to use a gun or sword so efficiently. There seem to be no reason for how she could mount a horse and fight the British.

How could a woman, whose life story shows no evidence of any military training or inclinations suddenly become a trained mounted warrior?

Thus, I conclude that the woman who fought in the *ghadar* is some other woman unrelated to the disciple of Haji Lal sahib.

There could be a slight suspicion that since this woman was descended from a family of soldiers bent on sacrifice, was influenced by the events of the *ghadar* and joined the rebel forces, she must have learnt horse riding and how to wield a gun and sword. It is possible that swayed by the spirit of sacrifice she went on to exhort and inspire the residents of Delhi to also fight along with her.

Or perhaps the rebel soldiers in charge made a crazed woman bent on sacrificing her life their stooge and taught her the skills needed for battle.

Nonetheless, whoever this woman was, she is one of the secrets of the universe and if those who write the history of the *ghadar* ignore her story, then they are guilty of leaving out a very interesting chapter of the *ghadar*.

In Asia and Hindustan, people with strong religious faith or at times those under some religious influence perform such mind-boggling, magnificent acts.

If that green-clad woman had got a chance to perform some other duty instead of just exhorting people into skirmishes, perhaps she would have become as famous as Chand Bibi, Raziya Begum and Nur Jahan.

I agree with Mr Hodson's letter that had the general not listened to Hodson's advice and had released that woman, she would have continued to trouble the British for a long time and it would not come as a surprise if she rekindled the fervour of the rebel soldiers to restart the fight against the British.

Another reason for my doubts is that those who are ordained into Sufism, do not believe it is legitimate to take part in struggles and wars against shariah. If she was indeed a disciple of Haji Lal sahib, why would she take part in a war like the *ghadar* which was against shariah? Perhaps she was misled like many other devout Muslims into thinking that the *ghadar* was actually a jihad.

I hope that if some British or Hindustani has come across the exploits of this green-clad woman and can furnish more details, then they should contact me so that I can note them down in the history of the *ghadar*.

Every Hindustani would like to remember, with pride, this woman's courage, determination and her military skills. I am sure they would like to know more about her so that Hindustan's pride stays high.[105]

---

105. There is no information on what happened to the woman after she was sent to Ambala jail.

22

The Grief-stricken Princess

The Present House of the Princess

The house had mud walls, one of which had collapsed in the last monsoon. There was a sackcloth curtain hanging on the door. When I called out, an old maid servant came to enquire and the princess allowed me to enter. The house had a very narrow courtyard where it must have been difficult to put cots. Even the lawn was so small that there seemed barely space to place a few cots. To the south of the lawn, there was a small storeroom.

When I entered, I saw the princess sitting on a coarse rug. There was a cot in the hall and in front of it, the princess was grinding some ingredients for her betel leaf in a small mortar. The rug was worn out and had many tears. There was a patched white sheet on the cot with a small and dirty pillow on it. There was a dusty *badhni*, earthen pot with a spout, kept in front of her which she used as a spittoon. A small betel box, clean but in need of polishing, was kept to her right.

The girders in the hall were old, and squirrels and mice had ruined them.

A Description of the Princess

The princess had completely white hair and even her eyelashes and eyebrows were white. She must have been tall in her youth which is why she had a stoop now. Her clothes were clean but patched. Her voice was clear, firm and sweet. Her Urdu diction was perfect and she spoke chaste Urdu. She spoke with great authority and dignity. Her face was wrinkled and her body frail.

Our Conversation

On entering, I greeted her with an *adab arz hai*, my salutations, and she responded with a *jeete raho*, may you have a long life. She continued, '*Miyan*, since my eyesight has become weak, I have not been able to come and pay my respects at the dargah sharif, the shrine of Hazrat Nizamuddin Auliya. I have never met you before, but I have heard your name often. When the old lady announced that Khwaja sahib had come to meet me, I was very happy that finally I could meet the person I have heard so much about. My ancestors had great faith in the shrine and I used to always attend the *satarvin*, *urs* ceremony. Now my eyesight is poor, and the weakness in my limbs doesn't allow me to move around.'

She continued, 'Tell me, why have you come here?'

I replied, 'I will just tell you the reason for my visit but first tell me if you are comfortable in this house. It is a very tiny house and the roof seems to have many holes in it through which dust must be coming in.'

She replied, '*Arrey Miyan*, what is there to worry about now? When fate forced us to leave the Qila and the palace, whatever we have is sufficient. What can be better than this house for which we pay a rupee and half as rent? Dust keeps falling from the roof and there's hardly any night when I don't have to clean the bedsheet. There was a time when I used to sleep in the Lal Qila and a bird had made her nest on its roof. A few twigs from it fell on my bed and I couldn't sleep the whole night. But now there is a constant stream of dust falling, yet I manage to sleep in it.'

I asked her, 'Do you get a pension from the government?'

She replied, 'Yes, I have been getting ten rupees a month for ages.'

I asked her, 'Do you have any other income?'

"Yes, I have a house from which I get a rent of seven rupees,' she said. 'I used to live in it earlier, but since I lost my eyesight, I could not make do with the pension I received. So, I put it on rent and came to stay here on a lower rental. We are two of us; this old lady and myself and we live comfortably in seventeen rupees and can meet the expenses of rent, food, my betel leaf and its condiments as well as the *nazar-niyaz*, offering of consecrated food to the poor.'

I said to her, 'I want you to describe your circumstances to me for my book, as I have written and published the stories of many men and women of your family.'

On hearing this she stopped grinding the betel leaf and said, 'No, *Miyan*, no. It is unacceptable to me that my name should become a cause for gossip in every house and lane.'

I replied, 'I will not publish your name, just your circumstances.'

She said, 'I have nothing to describe except this: we were once rulers and are now beggars.'

Beyond that she refused to say anything else except, 'Now, we will die.'

Her Story

I said again, 'Just tell me your circumstances, I will not reveal your name or address.'

The princess was very agitated by my words and for a long time she sat in stony silence. Then she prepared a betel cone for me and taking a deep sigh said, '*Miyan*, I was ten or eleven years old at the time of the *ghadar* and we lived inside the Qila. The emperor was angry with our branch of family but we got our monthly stipend regularly. I had three brothers and was the only sister. Though my mother was alive, my father had remarried in his old age. My mother and the new wife would fight frequently and my siblings and I also didn't get along with her. However, my stepmother was very fond of me and I was called the darling daughter of my stepmother and mother.

There were many male and female servants employed in our house to do the work. Just before the *ghadar* my stepmother died of cholera. Two of my brothers also fell prey to this disease. At the time of the *ghadar* there were just two of us siblings, and my respected father and mother.

The respected emperor left the Qila and went to Humayun's tomb. The rest of the residents of the Qila left soon after, and it was emptied quickly. Our mansion was away from the rest of the buildings in the Qila and built very strongly.[106] Abba Hazrat refused to leave. 'We will be killed even if we leave and that death will be ignominious. It is better to stay here. Whatever is written in our fate, it is better that it befalls us here,' he said.

For two days after the emperor left, no one came to our house. The servants had all run away and we had locked our doors. There were three-four doors with heavy iron chains at the entrance which we had secured. On the third day, we heard horse steps and people talking outside our house along with the sound of someone trying to break the main door.

My brother was sixteen years old. My parents both performed the *wuzu*, ablution, and told my brother to also do the same saying, '*Miyan*, get up, the time of death is near.'

I was very frightened when I heard these words and clung to my mother. She started crying and tried to pacify me saying, 'Don't cry. God is our helper and perhaps he will find some way to save our lives.' After that we all performed the *wuzu* and spreading out our prayer rugs recited our prayers and stayed in a state of prostration before Allah, supplicating him.

We could hear the door being battered down. We were still in a state of prostration when around ten or twelve white soldiers and

---

106. Apart from the main palace of the emperor, the princes had grand mansions inside the Red Fort. The descendants of past emperors, called *salatin*, also lived in houses and mansions inside the Red Fort.

ten or twelve Sikh soldiers, holding rifles with bayonets, entered our house.

Abba Hazrat and my brother stood up from their prostration and my mother, picking me up, hid my face with her chador.

One of the Sikh soldiers asked my father, 'Who are you and why are you here?'

Abba Hazrat replied, 'This is my house; I live here and am a descendant of Emperor Shah Alam.'

The Sikh soldier translated this for the benefit of the British officer. The officer questioned my father in broken Urdu which we didn't understand so the Sikh soldier repeated it to my father: 'sahib is asking that the *badshah* has fled, others have also fled, so why are you still here?'

Abba Hazrat replied, 'Our relationship with the emperor was estranged so he did not take us with him nor did we go along. We did not participate in the riots caused by the soldiers and we were convinced that the British government would not prosecute an innocent man. We did not flee as we are innocent.'

The British officer said, 'You will have to come with us to the ridge. We will investigate. If you are truly innocent, you will get immunity.'

Abba Hazrat replied, 'I have my wife and young daughter with me; there is no conveyance for them and they are not used to walking.'

The British officer replied, 'We can't organize a conveyance for you in the midst of this fighting. If you stay on here, some other soldiers may come and kill you ignoring your story. Therefore, you should leave as soon as you can. I will send two soldiers with you and if they see any vehicle on the way, they will put your wife and daughter in it; otherwise, you will have to walk all the way.'

Since there was no choice, Abba Hazrat reluctantly agreed. He took some expensive jewellery and gems, leaving everything else behind in the house, and we came out of the house with the soldiers. My mother was very frail and unwell so my father held her hand to help her, while my brother picked me up. We cast a look of longing at our beautiful home and left wondering if we would ever return. And that is what transpired. We never went back to it!

Once we came out, the British officers and Sikh soldiers mounted their horses and leaving two soldiers to escort us, rode off in the other direction.

Till the entrance of the Qila, the Sikh soldiers were content to wait and let my mother walk slowly as her body was trembling from the effort and she would sit down to rest after every ten steps. But once we were out of the Qila, they got irritated and asked us to hurry up saying, 'If we continue like this, it will be evening by the time we reach. Please walk faster.'

My father replied softly, 'Brother, you can see that my wife is ill and frail and she has never walked like this before in her life. We are constrained to walk slowly because of my wife and child, we are not being rebellious or disobedient.'

The soldier kept quiet on hearing this, but my brother couldn't control himself. 'You are from our country; don't you have any feelings of mercy for us?

One Sikh soldier replied, 'What can we do? We have to follow the orders of the ruler.'

My brother replied, 'The ruler has not asked you to be so harsh on us.'

The other soldier said, 'What harshness have we shown so far? However, now we will have to be harsh as you seem to be deliberately walking slowly.'

Saying this, one soldier came in front of us and the other behind us to force our pace. My mother got agitated on being forced to walk faster. She suffered from palpitations and she suddenly suffered an attack.

The Sikh soldier watched her quietly for some time then made a suggestion to my father, 'I will walk and can put your sick wife on my horse.'

My father picked up my mother and put her on the horse and with the soldier walking and my brother carrying me, we somehow reached the ridge.

The British forces were camped all over the ridge and we were put inside a tent. The Sikh soldier brought us some food from the mess and we passed the night.

The next day we were summoned by the general. He asked a local spy standing near him whether he knew us. The spy replied, 'Yes, I know him. He is a member of the emperor's family and he played a big role in the murder of the men, women and children inside the Lal Qila.'[107]

The general turned angrily towards my father. My father replied, 'This man is lying. He is a former employee of mine and I had him beaten up and dismissed from employment for the crime of stealing. He is now trying to take revenge. You ask him for how long I have been estranged from the emperor and have not paid my respects to him?'

The spy replied, 'While it's true that I was employed by him, he did not punish me or fire me because I was caught stealing. I left his employment of my own will because he did not pay well. And yes, it is true that his relationship with the emperor were strained but when the *ghadar* began he started visiting the emperor to get back into his good graces. The day the Britishers were murdered he and his son were present there and even argued with those who said that the murder of women and children was against Islamic teachings. He and his son said that killing the snake and leaving behind eggs and freshly hatched baby snakes was unwise. The women and children were killed because of their arguments.'

The general was enraged. Abba Hazrat kept reiterating that the spy was lying.

The general refused to hear anything further and gave orders that my father and brother be shot dead immediately. He added that, 'Though these two have murdered our women and children we will let his family be. Release his wife and daughter, let them go wherever they want.'

The Time of Execution

The soldiers came forward and caught my father and brother and tied their hands behind their backs. Abba Hazrat cast a glance

107. The massacre of British men, women and children by the sepoys on 16 May 1857.

at me and started crying but my brother stood silently. Amma Hazrat let out a long scream and fainted.

I ran forward to embrace my father but a soldier pushed me away and I fell on Amma Hazrat. I saw my father and brother being dragged far away by the soldiers to where some five or six soldiers stood with guns. The general was standing near them. He said something loudly which I didn't understand. After that he made some gesture in response to which the soldiers lifted their guns to their chest, ready to fire. I could hear Abba Hazrat calling out, 'I give you into God's care, my daughter for I am leaving this world.'

My brother called out, "Amma, Amma, my last salaam to you. Farewell.'

There was the sound of gunshots and I could see smoke. My father and brother were writhing in death's throes in the dust. I was crying in fright and my heart was sinking. When my mother regained consciousness I told her, 'They have killed my father and brother. See, there they lie writhing on the ground. Woe on me, Ammajan. Blood is pouring out of their chests. I have lost my father and brother and I will never see them again. My father had called out to me, while my brother called you. O Amma! What will happen next? Will they kill us too or will they imprison us?'

Amma propped herself on her elbows and gazed intently at my father and brother's bodies. They had stopped writhing and were absolutely still.

My mother called out piteously, 'My son! My darling! My sixteen-year-old love! My support, my husband has been snatched away from me. I have been ruined. I have nothing left in this world. O Allah, is this really happening or is it a nightmare? The blood-soaked bodies of my husband and my son are both lying in the dust. May the curse of God be on you spy for you have lied through your teeth. These two did not step out of the house since the *ghadar* started. What crime have you avenged by lying thus? You felt no pity for a sick woman or an innocent child? You have murdered two innocent men.'

Amma was still lamenting and wailing when the Hindustani soldiers came and caught hold of her and me and dragged us away. We passed by the two corpses and saw that their chests and faces was riddled by shots. Neither my mother nor I could walk but the soldiers were dragging us like goats. Our feet were torn by the rocky surface and were bleeding profusely. I don't know if anyone in the world experienced the kind of pain that we did that day!

The soldiers abandoned us to our fate once we were out of the army camp. My mother was lying unconscious while I sat next to her and kept crying.

After a while, a grass cutter passed by with a bundle of grass on his head. He put down his bundle and looked at my mother and said, 'This woman is dead.'

That man was a Hindu. He went into the army camp and brought back some Muslim grass cutters with him who confirmed his words, 'Yes, this woman is dead.'

They then proceeded to strip my mother and myself of all the jewellery we were wearing. 'Their men were carrying valuable jewellery and gems which have been confiscated by the army. But this jewellery is our right. They dug a hole and buried my mother. Two of them picked me up and took me towards Ajmeri Darwaza and left me there. I was sitting and crying there all alone when a Muslim goldsmith from Khanum ka Bazar passed by with his family. They were going to Qutub sahib, Mehrauli, and took me with them.

When peace returned to Delhi, the goldsmith family came back and handed me over to some princes from my family. I lived with them thereafter and got married to one of them when I reached the age of maturity. Later, my pension was fixed. God gave me many children but none survived. My husband passed away and in these past four years I have even lost my eyesight.

Have you heard enough, *Miyan*? This is the story of a poor distressed woman. Every pore of my body cries out in pain. I saw happiness only for ten years of my life and have spent the past seventy years suffering misfortune and bearing the blows of fate. I now sit with my feet in my grave, waiting for death.

I have found this old lady who stays with me and brings all the necessities for me from the market. We are both trying to get through these last days of our lives as best as we can.'

23

The Misfortunes of Nargis Nazar

Nargis Nazar was the daughter of Mirza Shahrukh[108] son of Bahadur Shah.

She was 17 years old at the time of the uprising of 1857.

In the present Red Fort of Delhi, between the Diwan-e Khas and Moti Masjid towards the west, and to the east of the garden there is a stone tank into which flows the *nahr-e bahist*. In its expanse is a beautiful palace.[109]

This marble tank had niches in it made for lamps over which the water from the stream fell like a chute into the tank. Mirza Shahrukh Bahadur lived in this Jal Mahal.

---

108. Mirza Shahrukh Bahadur had died in 1847. He was the heir apparent of the emperor and occupied an important status. The fact that he lived in the Jal Mahal, testifies to that. Nargis Nazar is most likely his granddaughter and there has been some mistake in the transcription of the story by the Khwaja.

109. Most of the mansions of the princes were destroyed after the fall of Delhi in 1857.This was probably one of the various apartments built in the area between the Diwan-e Aam and Diwan-e Khas, with the Moti Masjid as one boundary. A hauz, water tank, still exists in that area. A reference to apartments of the princes on the side of this hauz is given in *Qila-e Mualla ki Jhalkiya'n* by Arsh Taimuri. There is another Jal Mahal now called Zafar Mahal between the Sawn Bhadon pavilions in the Bagh-e Hayat Baksh on the other side of the Moti Masjid. This was built and used by emperor Bahadur Shah Zafar.

His wife had died, and he was very attached to his daughter.

It had been beautifully decorated with Kashmiri shawls, Turkish carpets and Banarasi brocades. Nargis Nazar had an aesthetic bent of mind and was a capable young lady. Her palace was the most magnificent amongst all the apartments and palaces in the fort and was always beautifully decorated.

Nargis Nazar's routine was such that she got up in the morning after sun rise. In summers, her canopied bed would be then taken into the courtyard which had a marble floor.

The legs and canopy of the bed were made of gold studded with gems. It was covered by a beautiful silk cloth. There were four soft and fluffy pillows with silk covers kept near the head of the bed along with two tiny bolsters on each side. These tiny bolsters prevented the princess' head from slipping from the pillow and saved her from waking up or facing any discomfort. Her cheek would automatically rest on them. Two slightly larger pillows were kept on the sides so that the princess could rest her knees on it. At night, when Princess Nargis Nazar went to sleep inside the canopy, flowers such as *juhi*, *mulsari* and *champa* would be kept next to the bolsters to make her bed fragrant throughout the night and make her repose pleasant.

When the princess lay in her bed, dancing girls would come and sing softly to help her fall asleep. In the morning, before the sun rose these dancing girls would come near the bed and sing the morning ragas in sweet voices to wake up the princess.

After getting up, the princess would stay in bed and keep yawning for a long time. The singing girls would make conversation with the princess.

One would say, 'Your highness, should I present a handkerchief for you to cover your mouth as you yawn?'

The other would say, 'The fishes in the pond are restless to see the sight of the princess stretching her limbs and jumping up to the surface of the tank.'

Nargis Nazar would rub her eyes and say with a smile, 'Go on, you liar. You are just making up stories.'

The girl would reply, 'Ask the mirror looking at you with such love whether I am saying the truth or lying.' She continued, 'It is trying to stroke your mussed up hair with its plump hennaed fingers and praise your beauty. One can see it is in a state of intoxication.'

The third would say, 'The red rays of the sun are emerging out of the clouds just like your highness' teeth peeping out from behind your red lips. Your cheeks are as luminous as the light of the true dawn. The scattered hair on your face resemble the black clouds gathering around the full moon, baring their emotions to the moonlight.'

Nargis Nazar would smile at these words and emerge from the canopy. She would relieve herself and wash her face with a scrub made of gram flour and other ingredients. After that her dress would be changed. Her toilette complete, she would eat her breakfast and turn her attention to decorating the palace. She would think up of new ways to make it look even prettier. The singers would return after lunch to entertain her. In the evening she would take a stroll in the garden.

The evening meal was always a grand affair with singers and dancers entertaining the princess as she ate with her courtiers and attendants.

The Last Night in the Qila

The night that Bahadur Shah left the Qila for Humayun's tomb and everyone was convinced that the British would capture the Qila the next day, Nargis Nazar stood at the edge of the Jal Mahal looking silently into the moonlit night.

Her reflection was falling on the water, and she was gripped by a strange mood, as if absorbed by her own image.

Suddenly, her father came and said, 'My daughter I want to go with my father. Will you come with me now or should I arrange a *rath* for you? You can come in the morning.'

Nargis Nazar said, 'Abbajan, please don't go now. Accompany me tomorrow. I don't think it is suitable for us to go with Dada Hazrat. The British forces are on the lookout for him and will treat everyone with him as criminals. It isn't advisable to go to

Humayun's tomb with him. Let us go to Ghazinagar,[110] where my milk mother lives. I have heard it is a safe place. We should adopt anonymity for now and can return once this calamity is over.'

The Mirza heard out his daughter and replied, 'As you say. I will arrange for conveyance to take us to Ghazinagar. Who will accompany you?'

'No one,' said Nargis Nazar, 'I will go alone for it is not prudent to take servants with us right now. The servants don't want to go with us.'

The Mirza left the palace to go and make arrangements. Nargis Nazar went back to staring at the moonlit water and her reflection in it.

After a while, she called out to her maid servants but there was no reply. She realized she was all alone in the Jal Mahal. This was the first time that no one answered her command, and she went into her palace in a flustered state. The candles were lit but there was not a soul in sight. Feeling frightened, she came back into the courtyard. She could hear voices coming from various parts of the Qila and it seemed as if people were leaving their houses. She stood there waiting for her father and when he didn't return for what seemed an eternity she started crying.

At around 2 a.m. at night a Khwaja-sara came and said to her, 'Sahib-e Alam has sent a message that British spies have spread out, in and outside the Qila looking for him. He can't go with you to Ghazinagar; however, he has arranged a *rath* for you and you should leave with me. He has said he will disguise himself and leave for somewhere else.'

Nargis Nazar cried out in perturbation, 'Oh, where does he intend to go?'

The Khwaja-sara replied, 'I have no idea.'

Nargis ordered the Khwaja-sara, 'Go and find out where Abba Hazrat intends to go and why he can't disguise himself and come with me to Ghazinagar?'

---

110. Modern day Ghaziabad

Nargis Nazar kept pacing up and down the courtyard. When the Khwaja-sara returned, he told her, 'Your Abba Hazrat has already left the Qila disguised as a stable hand, but I don't know where he is headed. And the *rath* is waiting to take you.'

Nargis Nazar started crying. This was the first time in her young life that she cried helplessly with hiccups and tears rolled uncontrollably down her cheeks. Once the storm of weeping was over, she took the box of jewellery and a few clothes which she gave to the Khwaja-sara to carry and left. Before she went further towards her conveyance, she took one last, long look at the beautifully decorated Jal Mahal and said, 'I don't know if I will ever see you again or I am being separated from you forever, today.'

It was 3 a.m. by the time Nargis Nazar sat in the carriage and set off for Ghazinagar. She reached Ghazinagar at 8 a.m. She had met many people and vehicles going up and down, but no one stopped her.

Her wet nurse's house was well-known in Ghazinagar and she reached there easily. As soon as her *rath* stopped, the wet nurse came running out to greet her. The wet nurse cracked her knuckles in front of her to ward of all evil from her foster child and took her inside with great care. She ensconced Nargis Nazar in her house and looked after the princess with care beyond her means.

The First Misfortune

Nargis Nazar lived comfortably for a few days in this house until news came that the emperor had been captured and many royal princes had been murdered. The British army was coming towards Ghazinagar to loot it.

Nargis Nazar asked the wet nurse to bury the jewellery box in the ground and waited for whatever trouble lay in store for her. After a while, the Sikh soldiers entered Ghazinagar and started searching for the rebels. Spies relayed the information that the emperor's granddaughter was living in the house of her wet nurse. Two Sikh officers and four soldiers came to the house and caught the wet nurse and her family. Nargis Nazar was hiding in the storeroom:

they broke open the door and dragged her outside. They made her stand, without her veil, with the rest.

The officer asked her, 'Are you the emperor's granddaughter?'

Nargis Nazar replied, 'I am an ordinary man's daughter. Had I been the emperor's granddaughter do you think I would be here in this simple house? If God had made me an emperor's granddaughter, why would you have brought me here without a veil in front of you? You are Hindustanis, don't you feel ashamed that you are oppressing the women of your country?'

The officer said, 'What oppression have we done? We are just enquiring who you are. We have heard that you are the granddaughter of Bahadur Shah and that your father had many British men, women and children murdered inside the Qila.'

Nargis Nazar retorted, 'As you sow so you reap. If you think my father has committed such a crime, you should question him. I have not committed any crime or killed anyone.'

Upon hearing this, the younger Sikh officer said, 'Yes you kill with your eyes! You don't need swords and weapons to murder anyone.'

Though Nargis Nazar had never spoken to a strange man before, she said with great courage, 'Quiet! One does not speak to royalty so discourteously. Your tongue will be ripped out of your mouth.'

The young Sikh officer was angered by these words. Coming forward to catch her by her hair, he pulled hard. The old Sikh officer restrained the young man and said, 'Don't behave so badly with a woman.' Reprimanded, the young Sikh officer let go of her hair.

They hired a bullock-cart and put Nargis Nazar on it. The wet nurse and her family were also arrested and made to walk beside it. The princess was asked, 'Where is your jewellery and money?'

She replied, 'I am a jewel myself and for those who look at me a treasure. I have nothing else.'

On hearing this the two officers kept quiet and took the cart towards Delhi. Near the Hindon river, the Jat and Gujjar villagers fired at the Sikh soldiers. The firefight continued for a long time. Since the villagers outnumbered the Sikh soldiers, the latter were all killed. The villagers arrested the prisoners and took them to their village. They stripped Nargis Nazar of whatever jewellery she was wearing and her expensive clothes and gave her a soiled and torn lehnga, kurta and dupatta to wear in exchange. Nargis Nazar wept uncontrollably and wore the clothes to cover her body.

Later, some Muslims from a nearby village came. Their headman bought Nargis Nazar from the villagers and took her with him. These people were Ranghars[111] and Tagas[112] by caste. The headman gave the offer of a marriage proposal for his son to her. Though they were villagers, he was a wealthy man, and the son was very good looking. Nargis Nazar accepted the proposal and the village *qazi* solemnised their nikah. She lived in great comfort for the next four-five months.

The Second Misfortune

The British were firmly in the saddle and their spies were roaming the countryside looking for 'rebels'. Someone informed the rulers in Delhi that though the rebel Mirza could not be found, his daughter lived in so and so village in the headman's house. The British sent a force to the village along with a posse of policemen from Meerut. They surrounded the village, arrested Nargis Nazar, her husband and her father-in-law and took them to Delhi. The British questioned Nargis Nazar for a long time but she could tell them nothing. Feeling dissatisfied with her answers, they gave orders that her husband and father-in-law would be called rebels as they sheltered a rebel's daughter. They would both be put in jail, while the woman would be handed over to a Muslim family in Delhi.

Consequently, the headman and his son were sentenced to ten-year prison each and Nargis Nazar was asked with whom she would like to live. The princess replied that if there was anyone from her family in Delhi then she should be sent to live with them.

---

111. Muslim Rajputs whose profession was agriculture
112. Despite Islam having established a classless society, the converted Muslims were often known and identified by the caste they or their ancestors had been born into.

On enquiry it was found that members of the Timurid family were either absconding or living in the jungles and villages. Since there was no one from her family living in Delhi, she was handed over to a Muslim soldier, who took her to his house.

This soldier was married. When the wife saw that her husband had brought a young and attractive woman with him, she beat him and pushed Nargis Nazar out of the house. This was the first time that Nargis Nazar had been pushed. The soldier came out of the house and took Nargis Nazar to a friend's house. The friend was an aged Muslim. When he heard Nargis Nazar's story, he started crying and lovingly gave her space to stay.

Nargis Nazar slept peacefully the first night. The next night as she slept a few men entered. Gagging her mouth, they kidnapped her. Nargis Nazar tried very hard to escape but their grip was so tight she couldn't move. These men belonged to the same village where Nargis Nazar had married the headman's son. However, they took her to another nearby village which belonged to the Taga Muslims. They put her inside a hut and gave her a cot to sleep on.

That cottage belonged to the village headman who was a kind-hearted individual. Nargis Nazar lived there for four years, doing all the housework. However, she could not milk the cows or make cow dung cakes.

Her husband was given an early release from prison. In four years, he came and took Nargis Nazar home. She spent the rest of her life with him bearing him many children. She died in 1911.

A Night of Trouble

Nargis Nazar used to say that when she lived with the Taga Muslims, one night during monsoons she had a very high fever. There were dark clouds and lightning everywhere while she slept on the bare cot wrapped in a cotton sheet. She dreamt that she was sleeping in her bejewelled golden canopy, enveloped in the smell of the *juhi*, *mulsari* and *champa* flowers, surrounded by soft pillows, the singing girls sing in a soft lilting tone all combining to give her a wondrous sense of ease and repose.

'I called out to one of the singers to help me get up. She came running and lifted me up on my pillows and while doing so mischievously poked me. I gave her a tight slap and she ran away laughing. I woke up from this dream and the memory of the Jal Mahal and its brightly burning lamps made me very restless. I came and stood at the door of my hut wrapped in the cotton bedsheet and watched the spectacle of the rain and the moon, lighting up the sky.

Ever since misfortune had befallen on me this was the first time that I felt restless. I had not yearned for the Jal Mahal or my previous royal life before this but for some reason that day I kept thinking that I was the granddaughter of the Emperor of Hindustan, my father's favourite, and till the age of seventeen I was a princess but now, I am a poor servant. I remembered the luxury and elegance of my palace when I was surrounded by beautiful things for my comfort whereas here I had to live in squalor and dirt and make do with coarse clothes and bedding. I had kept myself busy in making my palace and surroundings more beautiful. Later we secretly dug up the ground where I had buried my jewellery box in the wet nurse's house, only to find that everything had been stolen. God knows who took it all away. I had nothing left from my royal existence except myself and I had completely changed.

The restlessness that these memories caused made me dizzy and I fainted. I lay there in an unconscious state till morning. When I regained consciousness, I saw that I was in that small hut and there were hundreds of daily chores which I had to do and work harder than my slave girls ever had to for me!'

Khwaab tha jo kuch ke dekha,
jo suna afsaana tha

Whatever I saw was just a dream,
the rest is a fairy tale[113].

---

113. A verse by Mir Dard

24

The Kafni[114]

'Dilshad, don't tickle me. Let me sleep. What can I do if I am late for namaz? I don't feel like opening my eyes.'

'Bibi, I am not tickling you. This rose is brushing against your soles.'

'I will crush this rose. Why is it waking me up so early? I want to sleep. Call Sundari. Let her play Raag Bhairavi for me on her flute. Where is Gul Chaman? Let her come and massage my feet. You tell me a story.'

'If I tell you a story now, travellers will forget their way.[115] One should not tell stories during the day. Sundari is here and I am summoning Gul Chaman. If Ammajan comes, she will get angry that I haven't woken up Mah Jamal yet. It's getting past the time for namaz.'

Sundari was playing the flute when Mah Jamal opened her eyes. She tied her hair, smiled and read the *kalima*.[116] Nargis presented her salaam. In return, Mah Jamal pinched her, yawned and got up saying, 'Dilshad, I pinched Nargis but she didn't laugh and instead

---

114. An unstitched shirt worn by some faqirs. Also, an essential part of a shroud.
115. A reference to the belief that if stories were told in the morning, travellers would lose their way.
116. Islamic creed

made a face. Now you come here, Dilshad. I am going to pull your ears and you have to laugh loudly.'

Dilshad ran far away and said from afar, 'I am going to laugh loudly, you can imagine that you have pulled my ears.'

Mah Jamal smiled, got up and went towards the commode. She then performed her ablutions, read her morning prayers and came out into the courtyard. She sat down on a wooden settee near the garden and started reciting from the Holy Quran,

The serving maids were busy setting the carpet and *chandni*[117] on the floor. Once that was done they made preparations for breakfast.

After Mah Jamal finished her recitation of the Quran, the *maalan*, female gardener, came with green chillies in a straw basket. First, she took her hands near her face and cracked her knuckles, then took her fist to her face, in the traditional gesture off warding off evils, gave her blessings and said, 'Sarkar, today these chillies flowered in the royal garden. I have brought it to ward off the evil eye from yourself.'

Mah Jamal took the straw basket and called out to the serving maids. Soon the mahal was full of chatter about the advent of these green chillies.

Nargis said, 'Oh they look so smooth and green.'

Dilshad replied, 'Just like Bibi's cheeks.'

Sundari said, 'They are lying quietly in the basket just as Bibi sleeps in her canopied bed.'

Gul Chaman said, 'They have been broken off the bough and separated from the garden. That is why they are subdued.'

Mah Jamal ordered, 'Give a suit of clothes to the *maalan* along with five rupees cash. She has brought the first fruit from my tree. Give her a sweet to celebrate the occasion.'

The *maalan* was given a silken suit and a pair of silver bracelets. She was fed *laddoos*, given five rupees and prepared a betel leaf. She went off home after giving profuse blessings to Mah Jamal.

One of the serving maids went off to inform Ammajan, 'The first fruit from Bibi's orchard has arrived.'

---

117. White sheet

Ammajan came to her daughter from the neighbouring apartment, accompanied by her *mughlani*, attendant, and also warded off the evil from her daughter.

Mah Jamal said, 'Amma, *adab*.'

Ammajan and the *mughlani* praised the chillies, and for a while the chillies were the centre of attention.

Mah Jamal was the only child of Khurshid Jamal. Her father Mirza Ali Gauhar popularly called Mirza Nili, was the son of Shah Alam and the brother of Akbar Shah II. He had died ten years ago. Mirza Nili had many children from his serving maids, but only one daughter from his wedded wife, that too when he was quite old. Mah Jamal was only five years old when Mirza Nili died. She was now 15 years old by the grace of God. She had a dark complexion, medium height with an oval face and beautiful black drooping eyes which could intoxicate the beholder. Her voice was evocative and full of pain. Even when she spoke with a laugh, it seemed as if she was reciting a *marsiya*, elegy. The listener was struck by the anguish in it. She was mischievous, playful, pampered, sensitive and spoilt; brought up with a lot of love and attention. Obstinate and stubborn by nature, she was slim and when she walked her body bent naturally and swayed like a bough laden with flowers. As a result, she would stumble often and the serving maids would run along with her calling out, 'Bismillah, Allah we seek refuge and security from you.'

Phool Waalon ki Sair

Bahadur Shah had graced his new palace in Zafar Mahal, which was built near the gateway of the shrine of Khwaja Qutub sahib. The begums were inside but Khurshid Jamal and Mah Jamal had taken up a separate house on rent since they did not get along with Bahadur Shah, even when Mirza Nili lived. The British gave one lakh rupees every month to Bahadur Shah from which he sent one thousand rupees to Khurshid Jamal. Those were days when things were not so dear and one thousand rupees would be equal to a lakh today.[118]

---

118. The 'those days' here refer to 1922.

The evening when the *pankha*[119] was offered, Mah Jamal was sitting behind the curtain from afternoon itself. Trumpets were being played. The Hindu and Muslim residents of Delhi accompanied the *pankha*. Shops were decorated and the water carriers were clanging their silver cups to attract attention.

When it was time for the evening prayers, Khurshid Jahan, her mother sent the serving maids to call Mah Jamal to read her namaz then go back to enjoying the spectacle of the *pankha* procession. As Mah Jamal got up, she saw a faqir with a very pale face, bare feet, bare head, dressed in a white *kafni* or shroud. He passed by the *pankha* with his gaze on her. Mah Jamal was frightened by his face and shroud. She kept thinking of him even when she was reading her prayers.

When she finally went to sleep after the procession was over, she dreamt of the *kafni* many times. In the morning she woke up with a slight fever.

When the mother heard of it, she immediately read a few prayers for her daughter's health and sent charity to the faqirs. By afternoon, the fever was very high and Mah Jamal would keep waking up and start calling out to her mother, 'That man in the *kafni* has come, he is calling me. Ammaji, come and see, he is standing there smiling at me.'

The mother enquired what Mah Jamal was talking about from the servants. They told her, 'Yesterday, during the procession a faqir had passed by in a *kafni*. When Bibi got up for her prayers, the curtain was disturbed and the faqir stared at her and Bibi also saw him. After that he went away somewhere.'

Khurshid Jahan gave orders to her servants to search for the *kafni*-clad faqir.

The servants searched for him all over the fair. They found him in the evening and brought him to the house. Khurshid Jamal spoke to him from behind the curtain and described her daughter's state. He replied, 'Take me inside. I will read some prayers over her and she will recover.'

---

119. A fan shaped offering, made from flowers and profusely decorated with gold and silver.

Khurshid Jamal made arrangements for purdah and made the faqir stand next to the bed. The faqir closed his eyes, kept both his hands on his cheeks and stood quietly for a while. Then he said, 'Lo! The girl has recovered.'

They found that indeed the fever had abated. Khurshid Jamal and the serving maids were astonished. They asked the faqir to be seated and presented him with some money and two bolts of cloth. The faqir replied, 'I will not take all this. Show me the girl's face otherwise she will fall sick again.'

Khurshid Jamal was hesitant but then she thought to herself that faqirs are like parents and removed the curtain. Mah Jamal saw the faqir and bowed her head. The faqir saw Mah Jamal and kept staring at her. After a while he got up saying, 'May everything be well, Baba.' Then, he left.

The faqir was a young man of thirty but appeared to be sick. His face was pale and all he wore was the white *kafni*. His eyes were swollen as if from a storm of weeping. He was the son of the *maalan* who looked after the princess' garden.

He had seen Mah Jamal a year ago in the garden. Because of his poverty and Mah Jamal's position he did not have the courage to express the feelings that were clamouring in his heart after seeing her.

He spent six months in this state of agitation. Then, he met a Hindu *jogi* to whom he unburdened himself. The *jogi* gave him a white *kafni* saying, 'Wear this and your work will be done.'

After wearing the *kafni* he became semi-detached from the world and went into the jungle in a state of abstraction. For six months he roamed the jungles and had just come back into habitation when he saw Mah Jamal again. But now there was so much power in his gaze that Mah Jamal could not bear his gaze and fell sick with one glance.

After Fall of Delhi on 14th September 1857

On 14 September 1857,[120] a *rath* surrounded by soldiers from the British army in their khaki uniforms was standing near Najafgarh.

---

120. Most of the royals fled from the Red Fort after 17 May when the emperor himself had left. There may be some error in recall.

Khurshid Jamal, Mah Jamal and two serving aids were seated in that rath. Four servants were standing around the *rath* with drawn swords. The soldiers were insisting that they wanted to search the *rath* saying, 'It is harbouring some rebel sepoys.'

The begum's servants said, 'There are only women inside. We will not let you open the curtain.'

A skirmish ensued and the servants were all killed by the soldiers. When they opened the curtain, they saw the women. They snatched the box of jewellery as well as all the possessions that they were carrying and went away. The *rath* driver had fled. The begum took her charges and went towards Najafgarh when some Gujjars came and started demanding jewellery and clothes from them.

The begum said, 'The soldiers have already looted us and we have nothing left. You can take the *rath* and the bullocks.' But the Gujjars were not satisfied and forcibly removed their burqas. Except for their pyjamas they snatched away all their clothes. Khurshid Jamal and her maids started cursing them. One of the Gujjars hit Khurshid Jamal on her head with his stick while the others started raining blows on the maids. Mah Jamal was standing petrified. No one bothered with her. Khurshid Jamal's head burst open and she died thrashed on the ground. Mah Jamal was beside herself with fear. When she saw her mother dying, she started weeping. The Gujjars left after thrashing the women. Mah Jamal had fainted from the grief of her mother's death.

When she regained consciousness, she found that she was no longer in a jungle and her mother's and the maids' dead bodies had disappeared. She found herself lying on a cot. In front of her a cow was standing tied to a peg. A few hens were clucking in the courtyard and a Mewati[121] who was around forty-year-old, was sitting in front, talking to his wife.

Mah Jamal started crying and asked the wife, 'Where is my Amma?'

The woman replied, 'Your mother has died and we have buried her. We brought you here. Will you eat something? Look, I have made some kheer, please eat this.'

---

121. A Meo from Mewat region in present day Haryana

Mah Jamal said, 'I am not hungry,' and started wailing loudly with hiccups. The Mewatin tried to console her saying, 'Beti, you have to bear this with fortitude. What will crying gain you? Your mother can't be brought to life again. We don't have children and we will keep you here as our daughter. Think of this as your own house. Who are you? Who is your father and where were you going?'

Mah Jamal said, 'I am from the family of the *badshah* of Delhi. My Abbajan died eleven years ago. We set off from home in the stampede of the *ghadar*. Our gardener stays in Najafgarh and we were planning to take refuge in his house. On the way we were first looted by the soldiers and then by the Gujjars who killed my mother and our two serving maids.'

She started weeping again.

For some days Mah Jamal lived comfortably in the Mewatin's house though she would often remember her past and cry. The Mewatin's love ensured that she did not want for anything within their means. She would get her meals on time every day but kept longing for the luxuries of her past.

One night Mah Jamal, the Mewatin and her husband were sleeping when the thatched roof of the neighbouring house caught fire and spread to theirs. Mah Jamal woke up because of the acrid smell of fire and started shouting. The Mewatin and her husband ran into the house to retrieve some jewellery kept inside, while Mah Jamal ran outside. The burning roof fell down on the couple and they died in the fire. The villagers finally managed to douse the fire but Mah Jamal had lost her shelter and guardians.

In the morning the villagers buried the burnt corpses of the Mewatin and her husband. The *numbardar*, local chief, took Mah Jamal to his house. He had many children and two wives. They gave her a cot to sleep on. The next day one of the wives said, 'O you girl, put the milk on the fire to boil.'

The other wife called out, 'Come here, and put my child to sleep.'

On hearing two commands at the same time Mah Jamal was confused. She had never boiled milk or sung lullabies for any child. She picked up the earthen pot of milk to put on the wood stove but stumbled and fell. The pot fell from her hands and broke. The milk was spilt. On hearing the sound, the *numbardar*'s wife came running and slapped Mah Jamal, abusing her roundly.

Mah Jamal had never been slapped or abused before. She stood there shivering, alternately looking at her clothes drenched by the milk and the wife who was continuously abusing her.

Unable to take it any longer, she leaned against the wall and started weeping. Her tears further infuriated the *numbardar*'s wife who took off her slipper and hit Mah Jamal on her face. 'You are trying to scare me with your tears? You evil girl! Your inauspicious presence in their house, killed the Mewatin and her husband and now you have come to doom us. May God keep my children safe. Spilling of milk in front of the stove is considered very inauspicious. God knows what trouble your presence in our house will put us into!' she shouted.

Unable to bear the rain of slippers on her, Mah Jamal started crying loudly and hid her face with her hands. Meanwhile, the *numbardar* had also come into the house and hearing this commotion came to see what the matter was.

Mah Jamal ran and went to her cot. The *numbardar* also came out into the courtyard with his wife and asked her what was going on. When the wife related the incident he said, 'Doesn't matter. Let it be. It was a mistake. Have some consideration for this poor girl.'

The second wife called out, 'She is no innocent girl! She is a witch. I had asked her to sing a lullaby for my children but she ignored me and behaved as if she hadn't heard me. Have you brought her here to be a begum or a servant? If she has come as a servant then she will have to work.'

The *numbardar* replied, 'I have brought her here as an orphan. Of course, she should work. Anyway, we needed a maid servant.'

Mah Jamal replied with a tremor in her voice, 'I have never worked in my life. You teach me how to do the work. Destiny has brought me to this pass but it didn't teach me how to do any work. I had many serving maids and never needed to do anything myself.' The memories brought upon a storm of weeping and she started hiccupping.

The *numbardar* said, 'Don't cry. You will gradually learn.'

She was given some food. But unable to swallow a morsel, Mah Jamal went to sleep hungry.

In the morning, one of the wives shook her hard saying, 'O you lazy girl! When are you going to get up? It is time to sweep the floor.'

Memories of Dilshad, Nargis and Sundri waking her up came flooding into the young girl's mind. She got up with a long sigh and as per her habit yawned languorously.

The wife pushed her saying, 'You want to spread ominousness in my house and not get up?'

Mah Jamal was hit with the realization that she was no longer a princess and had really become a serving maid. She got up immediately but tears fell continuously from her eyes.

The other wife said, 'This woman can't last in our house. She cries all the time. We can't keep such an inauspicious woman in a house where there are children.'

The *numbardar*, hearing his wives' incessant complaining, threw Mah Jamal out of their house.

She was standing in a shock wondering what to do when she remembered the *maalan*, who lived in this same village and at whose house her mother had planned to take shelter in.

While Mah Jamal was wondering what to do, the faqir in the *kafni* happened to pass by. He was horrified to see Mah Jamal standing there in this condition.

Even though she was in so much trouble, the sight of the faqir in his *kafni* and his pale face, red eyes affected her deeply. A strange tremor ran through her body.

The faqir asked, 'How come you are here, my queen?'

When Mah Jamal heard the word 'queen' she turned her face away in deference. 'Destiny has brought me here,' said Mah Jamal and then related the entire chain of events to him.

The faqir replied, 'I live close by but I didn't get any news of you. Please come to my house.'

Mah Jamal followed him to his house. The faqir went inside and narrated the story to the *maalan* who came running out. Seeing the princess, she fell on her feet crying uncontrollably. 'May I be ransomed over you,' she said repeatedly.

She took Mah Jamal in with all due respect and ensconced her on the wooden cot in their house. She asked her about the circumstances that brought her to this pass.

'Begum this house is yours. I don't have anyone except my son. It is because of your family's benefaction that today I am prosperous. From today you are the owner of this house and my son and I are your servants,' the *malaan* said.

The *maalan* did whatever was within her capability to make Mah Jamal as comfortable as possible and soon the princess forgot her woes.

Mah Jamal saw that sick people from far and wide come to get healed by the *maalan*'s son. The faqir would rub his hands on his *kafni*, keep his hands on his cheeks and close his eyes for a while, and then opening them would say, 'Go, you have been healed.'

And truly, all their diseases disappeared and they were healed.

After a few days of observing this, she asked the *maalan*, 'How did your son get these powers? Once he had healed me like this as well.'

The *maalan* folded her hands and said, 'If I can ask for your indulgence and beg for the safety of my life, I can tell you.'

Mah Jamal said humbly, 'I am in no position to give any guarantee for anyone's life. You say what you have too. I am very curious to know the secret.'

The *maalan* said, 'Begum, my son had fallen passionately in love with you and underwent many trials because of his separation from you. Finally, he met a mendicant who gave him this *kafni*. It is the blessings of that faqir and this *kafni* that he can heal others. And God has now sent you here too!'

Mah Jamal was greatly impressed by the *maalan*'s words. She thought over them for many days. Eventually she asked the *maalan* to call the Qazi sahib who solemnised her nikah with the *kafni*-clad faqir.

The *maalan* looked after Mah Jamal with such love and affection all her life that Mah Jamal would say, 'I have forgotten my childhood.'

The *maalan*'s son never gave up his *kafni* and his fame spread far and wide.

Even Mah Jamal's tragic life had once again returned to happiness.

25

Mirza Mughal's Daughter, Lala Rukh

In the *ghadar* of 1857, the rebel soldiers appointed Mirza Mughal, the brave and strong son of Bahadur Shah, as their commander-in-chief. Mirza Mughal started discharging his duties as their leader.

One day 49 British women, men and children were murdered in the Lal Qila because of the villainy of the rebel forces[122]. When these British men, women and children were herded together in front of the Diwan-e Khas, to be murdered, Mirza Mughal was watching this spectacle from the roof of his mansion. His eight-year-old daughter Lala Rukh was standing beside him. She saw that even children were brought to be slaughtered, and that they were crying desperately while their mothers clutched them and pleaded to God for their children's life on bended knees. There was not a single eye that was not wet with tears and Lala Rukh too, began to weep.

Some of Mirza Mughal's courtiers who accompanied them, especially, his daughter's tutor Maulana Ainullah sahib said, 'Sahib-e Alam this is an act of great cruelty. No religion approves of the

---

122. On 16 May 1857 the rebel sepoys massacred 49 Europeans and British, mainly women and children in front of Red Fort's Naqqar Khana. There are other accounts such as Dastan-e Ghadar , an eye witness account by Zahir Dehlvi, which describe the emperor's efforts to prevent it, saying it was against the tenets of Islam to slaughter innocents. However, the sepoys ignored all pleas.

murder of women and children and Islam has especially forbidden it in very strict terms. *Lillah*, for God's sake, ask these soldiers to spare the women and children.'

Mirza Mughal replied, 'Undoubtedly, this is an act of oppression and tyranny. However, it is not easy to control the ignorant soldiers and the angry officers. They are totally out of control and have lost their sense of decency. Ever since they rebelled against the English, they have become so wilful and wild that they do whatever they want and refuse to listen to anyone's orders.'

Maulana Ainullah sahib replied, 'They have appointed Sahib-e Alam as their commander-in-chief and they have accepted Jahanpanah Zill-e Subhani Aala Hazrat Badshah Salamat. Why won't they listen to your orders or your father's? You should try to make them obey you. Can't you see that the wails and cries of these British women and children is shaking the skies?'

Mirza Mughal replied, 'Maulana, my father and I are mere puppets. The truth is that they listen to neither me nor the Hazrat Badshah Salamat. When these British men and women were arrested, I had sent them to the Lal Qila to be under the protection of the Hazrat Badshah Salamat so that their lives could be spared. But even inside the Qila, these cruel rebels kept the English men and women under their control and did not listen to any intervention by the emperor. So much so that when he sent food from the royal kitchens for the prisoners, they resisted and it was with great difficulty that they agreed to let them eat.

'They think that the emperor and his progeny are conspiring with the English against them. As a result, their sepoys have often confronted me and Jahanpanah saying, "We have jeopardized our families and ourselves, yet you don't appreciate what we are doing. In fact, you keep taking their side on every issue. If this continues then we will first kill you with our swords."

'Maulana, I ask you in all fairness to tell me how can I negotiate with such a murderous and rebellious group? If I try to prevent them from killing these English men and women, they will take me and my family to this same spot where these prisoners have been rounded up, and murder us first.'

Maulana Ainullah said, 'Sahib-e Alam, your helplessness is justified but Islam commands that even if one's life is at stake one must help the oppressed. This world is transient. Come, come with me. I will go and admonish these rebels myself.'

Mirza Mughal did not give any reply but from his expression it was clear that he was influenced by the Maulana's words. However, before Mirza Mughal could say a word, a man who was standing behind the courtiers came running and stabbed Maulana Ainullah in the back and ran away and hid amongst the rebel soldiers. The knife had pierced through Maulana's ribs and cut his kidney into half, killing him immediately. Before the poor Maulana could get a chance to reason with the sepoys, he passed on to the next world.

Lala Rukh was frightened by this incident and initially shocked into silence at seeing the murder of her teacher. After a while she started weeping calling out, 'Oh my poor Maulana.'

The rebel forces ran away and the British forces captured Delhi. The emperor was captured from Humayun's tomb. Mirza Mughal, Mirza Abu Bakr and some other princes were captured by the victorious forces and killed.

Lala Rukh, along with her mother Manzoor Nazar, who was a concubine of Mirza Mughal set off towards the jungle in a bullock-cart. The two women were accompanied by a servant called Khanum. Amongst the men with them were Mirza Ghasita, a distant relative of Shah Alam, and Mirza Mughal's employee, Qudrat Khan.

The bullock-cart had crossed Qutub sahib's dargah and was headed towards Chattarpur when a group of cavalry men appeared. Thinking that the British forces had arrived, they decided to go to the side and hide among the bushes. But before they could make any progress, the cavalrymen caught up with them and surrounded the bullock-cart.

Lala Rukh saw that the man who had killed Maulana Ainullah was also in this group. She whispered in her mother's ears, 'This isn't the British force. They are the rebel sepoys.'

The horsemen said, 'Give us all your valuables.'

Mirza Ghasita recognized one of the rebel sepoys and said, 'You should be helping us not looting us!'

On hearing this Maulana Ainullah's murderer said, 'You people are not worth helping. Your spies helped the British gain victory and we had to flee.'

Qudrat Khan retorted, 'That is not true. You did not obey us, and despite such a large force you fled and destroyed our comfortable life too.'

These words angered the rebel soldiers immeasurably and they attacked the carriage driver and the two other men with their swords. Very soon the driver, Mirza Ghasita and Qudrat Khan lay dead. Khanum Bai tried to save Qudrat Khan and lost her life in the process.

The rebel sepoys looted everything inside the cart going to the extent of stripping the corpses of their clothes. All the valuables Lala Rukh and her mother had carried were snatched away. They even forced the two to take off all the jewellery that they were wearing.

Next, they started debating who would get to keep the women.

One rebel said, 'The woman is young, I will marry her. Give her to me and in exchange you can keep all the jewellery that is my share.'

Maulana Ainullah's murderer said, 'I don't have children, I will take the girl.'

Thus, were the two divided amongst the rebels. The rebel soldier made Lala Rukh's mother sit behind him on his horse, while Maulana Ainullah's murderer put Lala Rukh on his.

Lala Rukh started wailing for her mother and Manzur Nazar asked the rebel sepoy to take her daughter along with them too, so that they could be together.

The rebel soldier said, 'I am a resident of Bharatpur and that is where I will take you. The other man lives in Sohna, district Gurgaon, and that's where he will take your daughter. We don't want to disturb the division of spoils.'

Lala Rukh's mother pleaded and cried for mercy, 'Don't separate me from my only daughter.' But the tyrants felt no pity for her. The Bharatpur sepoy took Lala Rukh's mother to his home while Maulana Ainullah's murderer took the daughter to Sohna.

Lala Rukh's Story

Lala Rukh narrated that when she and her mother were separated, her mother kept pulling her hair and wailing loudly, as did she.

I kept calling out, 'Amma, Amma!'

However, our cries had no effect on the hard-hearted tyrants.

I kept crying out for my mother as long as I could see her horse, after that I fell silent.

In Sohna, that man took me to his house. He was a *ghosi*, cowherd, by caste and there were three to four buffaloes tied next to his house.

When his wife heard that he had adopted me and brought me, she was delighted and made me sit near her with great love and affection. The *ghosi* and his wife pampered me so much for the next eight days that I forgot the pain of separation from my mother. On the eighth day a British force came and arrested my 'new' father. They also confiscated everything in the house.

My *ghosan* mother tried to pacify me and took me to a neighbour's house. After three days we heard that the *ghosi* had been hanged for the crime of rebellion and his house and possessions would be auctioned.

That poor *ghosan* had taken enough cash from her house while fleeing that she could live off it for two years. In this period, she left no stone unturned to care for me.

One day some thieves broke into our house and wanted to take off the *hansli*, necklace, that my *ghosan* mother was wearing. She woke up and started shouting. To stop her, the thieves strangled her and she died from suffocation.

After my *ghosan* mother died, the family we were living with kept me for three or four days, then the wife started complaining, 'You keep sitting around the whole day. Why don't you do some work. We are not running a free kitchen and you will only get food if you work.'

I asked her, 'Tell me what work to do. I will do it.'

She replied, 'Sweep the house, clean the buffalo dung and make cow dung cakes from it. Every day.'

I replied, 'I don't know how to make cow dung cakes or sweep. I have never done any work. I am the granddaughter of the emperor of Hindustan. However, fate has brought me to this pass and I will do whatever you tell me. Show me how to do all this a couple of times so that I may learn.'

That woman was very kind hearted and she taught me how to sweep and make the cow dung cakes and soon I started doing the work.

One day I had very high fever and was lying in bed when her husband came and seeing me asleep kicked me and said, 'It is ten o'clock and you are still sleeping? This is not the Lal Qila but a *ghosi*'s house. Get up and do your work.'

I got up with tears in my eyes and said, 'Forgive me, I have erred. I will immediately finish my work.' Thus, in my sick state with high fever, I swept the house and made the cow dung cakes.

At that time I was naïve, but now when I think about my troubles my heart gets restless. I keep reflecting on the troubles that we had to go through because of the actions of those rebel sepoys.

We were residents of the palace whose grandeur and beauty were incomparable. We made poets write wondrous verses in its praise.

The walls of the palace had this verse inscribed on it:

Agar firdaus bar ru-ye zamin ast
Hamin ast-o hamin ast-o hamin ast

If there is heaven on earth
It is this, it is this, it is this!

But destiny has brought us suffering and now we have to roam like nomads searching for shelter and make cow dung cakes to survive.

After living like this for two years the *ghosi* married me off to his brother and that is where I spent the rest of my life. I deliberately tried to forget my royal life in the Qila but I was helpless before my restless heart. It would keep throwing up memories. I would dream of my father Mirza Mughal ensconced on his royal *masnad* with my head on his knees. Serving maids stood around, fanning us, and the world was a piece of heaven. But as soon as I woke up all I could see was a thatched roof, a millstone and three cots.

Today if someone asks me if I am Mirza Mughal's daughter, I will reply, 'No! I am a poor *ghosan*, for a person's caste is decided by the work they do.'

26

The Woman Who Gave Birth During the Ghadar

When Nawab Faulad Khan's corpse was brought home from the ridge, his daughter-in-law was in the throes of labour pain.

At that time there was no house in Delhi which was not either escaping from the city or getting ready to escape. It was being openly said that Bahadur Shah had left the Lal Qila and gone to Humayun's mausoleum.

Faulad Khan was a hereditary nobleman but for some reason his father had incurred the displeasure of Akbar Shah II and had been stripped of his *mansab* and *jagir*. Faulad was a young man at that time and took up employment in the British army. When the sepoys rebelled, he too joined them. On the last day he went to attack the British positions on the ridge with his regiment. He fought very bravely until he was struck down by shrapnel from a cannon ball and lost his life.

When the sepoys brought his body home, they saw that his daughter-in-law was writhing with labour pain and there was no midwife to help with the baby's delivery.

Faulad Khan's young son had been killed four days earlier. Her mother-in-law had died two years ago. The recently widowed daughter-in-law was now without any support. Her lone guardian, her father-in-law also lay dead. Seeing his lifeless body drenched in blood, eyes closed and wearing the finality of death on his face, Sakina Khanum's world went black.

There was every material comfort in the house, including four maid servants but the comfort of a guardian had been snatched away from her. Sakina Khanum cried out loudly and fainted from shock.

Faulad Khan's body was laid out in the courtyard and the sepoys were waiting by the door. Sakina lay unconscious on her bed. Two maid servants were sitting at the head of the bed and two towards the bottom. All four were in a state of shock, weeping uncontrollably.

After a while Sakina regained consciousness as the labour pain increased. Grappling with the pain she asked one of the maids, 'Go and see if there is any sepoy still standing in the *deorhi*. Ask him to go and search for a mid-wife.'

The maid went to the door and came back running, wailing loudly, 'Bibi, the angrez khaki,[123] have arrested the sepoys and are taking them away. Some khaki-clad British soldiers are approaching our house too.'

Sakina shouted, 'Quickly close the door, you wretch.'

The maid went back running and closed the main door of the house.

The labour pains increased. There was no midwife or help available, but nature itself decided to ease her trouble and Sakina gave birth to a boy. Sakina had once again fainted from the shock and pain. The maids bathed the baby and wrapped him in some clothes and one of them sat near the mother with the baby in her lap.

Sakina was seventeen years old and had been married a little over a year ago. Her own family lived in Farrukhabad and she was all alone in Delhi facing these tumultuous events.

When she gained consciousness, she asked her maid, 'Give me some support so that I can sit up.'

The maid replied, 'Don't even think of sitting up Bibi. It will be very harmful for you. Keep lying down, you don't have the strength to sit up right now.'

---

123. The British soldiers were referred to as khaki during the *ghadar*.

'Don't be foolish Bua,' said Sakina. 'This is not the time for such niceties and caution. We have no idea what else destiny has in store for us.'

The maid helped her sit up, propping her up with a bolster. Sakina looked at her baby with eyes full of maternal love and wanted to keep gazing at her most precious desire, but after a while she felt shy. She smiled and turned her gaze away. Her happiness soon turned into sorrow for her eyes fell on Faulad Khan's body lying in the courtyard. The shock made her delirious and she started saying:

'See your orphan grandson! Get up, the one whose birth you so desired has been born. You had cuddled his father, now get up and cuddle the son. How will I take care of this child? I am helpless and without any support. This poor baby has no idea that the house he has been born in is caught up in so much trouble.

'You were my guardian in Delhi, now you have also died. My own father is in Farrukhabad but he has been separated from me. This baby too had a father, who was my whole world but he has been killed by a gunshot.'

Sakina was overcome with grief on remembering her husband. Cradling her head with her hands, she started weeping uncontrollably. The frenzy of weeping exhausted her and she fainted again.

The maid ran outside to see if she could find someone to bury Faulad Khan. She found the lane outside the house deserted. Not a single person could be seen around. She gestured to the second maid and said, 'Bua let us run away and save our lives. If we stay with Bibi, are lives are in danger too.'

The second maid replied, 'To betray someone in such a difficult time, to think about saving my life, would be the most disloyal and inhumane act. And you forget there is the question of a poor helpless baby.'

The first maid answered, 'Don't be crazy. At such a time there is no scope for thinking of loyalty and humanity. If one survives, one can have the world. I am off. You decide what you want to do. The soldiers will be arriving any minute, they will loot the house and kill all of us.'

This alarmed the other maid, whose heart hardened. She gestured to the third and fourth maid who were also ready to run away. These two said, 'If we are running away, let's take some money for our expenses. Sakina is unconscious and the bunch of keys is kept near her head. Let's take the safe with cash box from the storeroom with us.'

The maid who was holding the baby said, 'Who will look after this baby?'

One maid said, 'Leave him next to the mother.'

'No, I think I will take the baby with me, otherwise who will look after him?' she said.

'God be praised! Here we have no idea how we will survive and she wants to take a baby with her too! Apart from that this will devastate Sakina and kill her. Have some mercy on her.'

'You are a nice one to talk! You yourself feel no mercy at leaving Sakina alone and you are pointing fingers at me. I will take this baby and give him to my daughter. She recently lost her baby and she will bring up this infant,' said the maid holding the baby. 'If I leave this baby behind, it will die with Sakina.'

The four maids stole the cash box from the store room and taking the new born baby, left for their houses. Sakina was left all alone in the house with her father in law's body.

She lay unconscious for four hours from the shock of Faulad Khan's death and weakness from the delivery.

She regained consciousness at eight in the night to find herself in a pitch-dark house. Finding no one around, she thought that she had died and reached the darkness of the grave.

She instinctively started reading the *kalima*, Islamic creed, and testifying: 'There is one God, Mohammed is his Prophet and my faith is Islam,' and 'I am innocent please take me from the dark grave into the light of heaven.'

When she saw the twinkling stars in the sky, she realized that she was alive and lying on her bed she started calling out to the maids. When no reply came, forgetting her frail and weak state she got up, lit a candle and found that she was all alone in the house with her father-in-law's body.

The sight of the dead body at night scared her and she started shouting in panic. There was no one to hear her shouts and come to her aid. Sakina was now screaming in a total state of panic and fear overcame her. Once again, she fell down unconscious on the floor.

She remained unconscious till mid-morning. When she opened her eyes, she found some strength in her heart. Though she hadn't eaten anything for two days and had to bear so many shocks to her heart and body, she had been brought up in a military household and had more courage than most women. She decided to bury her father-in-law's body. Before that she wanted to eat something as she was very hungry. Just then she remembered her baby. Where was he? As soon as this thought occurred, her maternal instincts came to the forefront and she ran around the house like a crazed woman searching for her baby. When the baby was nowhere to be found she lifted the lids of the earthen pots of water peering in them to check if the infant was there. She pulled away the pillows from the bed and started cuddling them.

Finally, her grief subsided and she once again found some fortitude in herself. Once again, she turned her attention to the issue of burying her father-in-law. She found a white sheet in the almirah and covered the martyr's body with it. Spreading out her prayer rug, she fell down in prostration. She wept and called out loud, 'O God, this is the corpse of one of your creatures who has neither a shroud nor a grave, there is no one to read his funeral prayers. Send your angels to read his funeral prayers and bury him in their embrace of mercy. I have been betrayed by everyone. My husband has left me and lies in the grave, my darling has been snatched away from me, and I have no other support apart from you. Please accept this prostration of helplessness and hold my hand.'

Sakina was still prostrated when the door opened and four khaki-clad soldiers came inside. She raised her head and seeing strangers, covered her face with her chador. She tried to move away into a corner but the soldiers were already close by. They caught her and forcibly removed her chador from her face. They all said in unison, 'She is young and so beautiful.'

After that they left her and started scouring the house for things to loot. Cash had already been taken away by the maids, but they found some jewellery and expensive clothes which they took.

They lifted the sheet from Faulad Khan's face and said, 'Oho! This seems like an important rebel.'

They then lifted Sakina up forcibly and said, 'Hey you! You come with us.'

Sakina was helpless and let herself be lifted. She stood there silently unable to say that, 'I am a new mother, I am hungry.'

Modesty and embarrassment at her predicament prevented her from saying that I have no one in this world to speak up for me. Don't molest me.

She sighed in great distress when the soldiers dragged her till the door and turning back to look at her house she said, 'Farewell! O house of my in-laws. Farewell, you shroud-less unburied corpse. I am the pride of these swordsmen. Had they been alive, they would have died defending my honour.'

The soldiers laughed when they heard these heart-breaking words of Sakina. They dragged her outside. For some time, Sakina walked silently. Then, she said, 'I have recently given birth, please have mercy on me. I am hungry, have some pity for me. I am your fellow country woman, I am from the same faith as you and I am innocent.'

Hearing this the four soldiers stopped in their track and said in an apologetic tone, 'Don't worry we will bring a carriage for you.' One of them brought a cart in which wounded were carried and put Sakina in it. They took her to the camp on the ridge.

Twelve Years Later

No one knows what trials and tribulations this new mother went through during these twelve years. When I saw her, she was begging in a locality in Rohtak. She was bare foot, wearing a dirty patched kurta and a torn pyjama. Her head was covered by a torn rag of a dupatta. She looked malnourished and her bones were sticking out of her skin. She had dark circles under her eyes and uncombed hair. Though she had been looted of her life, her face still retained its beauty. Her eyes still had their natural beauty but looked desolate and haunted. She stumbled as she walked and stopped to take support from the wall, took a deep breath and walked forward.

A few steps ahead, she found a house where a wedding was being held. Hundreds of people were coming out after eating. She went and stood there and let out a heart-rending call:

'I am from a noble family and have been tormented by fate. I have lost my chastity and forgotten my modesty and come to ask for a morsel to eat. May your bride and bridegroom be safe from all calamities, and their marriage prosper, give me a bite to eat as a propitiatory offering, sahib.'

No one heard this piteous cry in the clamour made by the beggars. In fact, one servant inadvertently pushed her so hard that she fell down flat on her face. She cried out, 'I have not eaten anything for three days. Don't beat me for fate itself has beaten me. O God, where do I go? Who will hear my sorry tale and offer me succour?'

She started crying. A boy standing nearby heard her and seeing her, also started crying. He helped Sakina get up and said, 'Come with me, I will get you some food.'

With great difficulty Sakina managed to go with him. He was a servant in a nearby house. Food had come for him from the wedding house and he put his share in front of her. Sakina ate a few morsels and as she gained some strength started blessing the boy.

When she saw the boy closely, a storm of feelings awoke in her heart. She clutched him and started crying uncontrollably. The boy also felt some yearnings in her embrace.

Sakina asked him, 'Whose son are you?'

The boy replied, 'My mother is a maid servant in this house and I also work here.'

Sakina asked, 'Where is your mother?'

The boy answered, 'My mother and my grandmother have both gone to the wedding with the mistress.'

Sakina fell silent but she wondered why there was an out pouring of love in her heart for this boy? Yes, he had been kind to her but kindness doesn't inspire such emotions.

Just then the boy's mother and grandmother returned. Sakina immediately recognized the grandmother as her former maid servant who had run away with her baby during the *ghadar*. The maid servant didn't recognize Sakina but when Sakina called out her name and identified herself, she caught hold of Sakina and started weeping frenziedly.

Soon, the boy came to know that Sakina was his real mother. He embraced her tightly and wept tears of joy. Sakina looked up at the sky and said, 'I offer thanks to you, O God, my cherisher. I am in your debt my Lord that you kept my baby alive during the death and destruction of the *ghadar* and you have turned my days around after twelve years of sorrow.'

After that Sakina got a letter sent to her family in Farrukhabad. Her father had died since but her three brothers were alive. They came to Rohtak and took their sister and nephew back with them. The boy insisted to take the maid servant and the daughter who had brought him up along with them.

In Farrukhabad, they started living a life of ease and luxury.

27

The Last Cup of Wine[124]

When the cup bearer still held the cup, Delhi was hosting soirees and Prince Gul-Andam was alive. An intoxicated wine drinker had said, 'Friends! This is the last night. Thank your stars that tonight a few like-minded people are gathered together. There will be nothing left here tomorrow!'

I

At that time Prince Gul-Andam stretched himself languorously and said, 'Why are you spoiling this assembly today with gloomy forecasts of the morrow? Bahadur Shah has left the Qila and tomorrow the British forces will enter. The time we have tonight is a boon. Keep sorrow away for a few more moments. O cup bearer pour out another cup of wine for me so that I may enjoy this evening one last time.'

Morning was near and the cannons on the ridge were continually shelling shaking Delhi to its very foundations.

---

124. This was published in the Urdu magazine *Saqi*, in November 1930. The magazine was edited by Shahid Ahmad Dehlavi and printed at Delhi Printing Works, Delhi.

II

A few young men were gathered in a palatial house in Khas Bazar. The sounds of a sitar playing could be heard from afar. Candlesticks and baskets full of flowers were kept all over the room, burning brightly with wax melting down their sides.

Prince Gul-Andam was a close relative of Emperor Bahadur Shah. The organizer of this assembly was a young man from the family of Nawab Gulroo of Jhajjhar.

Everyone was convinced that tomorrow Delhi would be conquered. The emperor had left for Humayun's tomb and the British would enter the Qila in the morning. Thus, they had arranged an assembly to enjoy one last night of luxury and enjoy their empire.

Tharthari, a man with a sweet voice and pleasant demeanour was made the cup-bearer. Verses which were dripping with pathos and a sense of doom were being recited and thoughts of death were on everyone's mind.

Everyone got up to leave as dawn broke and Gul-Andam's servants informed him that his *rath* was at the door. Gul-Andam awarded the man who had enacted the role of cup-bearer, embraced Gulroo, saw him off and then himself left for Alwar.

III

After fifteen days, news spread in Alwar that spies had come looking for the relatives of the emperor as well as those who had participated in the *ghadar*.

Gul-Andam was strolling on the roof. He was dressed in a fine muslin kurta, fanning himself with a hand fan. A few people entered without permission and said, 'Sahib-e Alam, you are under arrest. Come we have brought a conveyance which is waiting downstairs.'

Gul-Andam smiled and got into the *rath* which set off for Delhi. There were some seven or eight other *raths* carrying prisoners to Delhi but none seemed sorrowful; they were cheerfully chatting with each other.

IV

There were chairs kept in front of Sunehri Masjid in Chandni Chowk.[125] British men and women were sitting in front of the gallows erected there. The prisoners were standing trussed up; they were brought one by one and hanged to death.

Gul-Andam was also brought. Dressed in a fine muslin kurta and embroidered slippers, he retained his nonchalant style. His fair smiling face, broad chest, slim waist, big grey eyes and cheerful demeanour prompted the officer sitting there to ask him, 'Prince Gul-Andam! You are accused of participating in the rebellion and that is why you are being hanged.'

Gul-Andam turned around. Looking the officer in the eye he said, 'I had nothing to do with either the rebellion or the submission to the government. Yes, I am a sinner in the eyes of God. I used to drink and offer wine to others; I had divorced myself from reality and the sorrows faced by the people around me. You say that I have participated in rebellion! Yes, I rebelled against God and I deserve whatever punishment I am given.'

Hearing this speech, the officer gestured to a police constable, who took Gul-Andam to the gallows and tied the noose around his neck.

Suddenly a scream pierced the air and everyone turned towards it. It came from the crowd standing nearby. An old woman was crying uncontrollably and repeatedly calling out, 'My son, my Gul-Andam!'

Gul-Andam had just turned around to look at his mother when the plank was pulled, and he was hanged to death.

The constables wept at the old lady's anguish and pain filled voice. Even the officer's eyes filled with tears.

V

By 1930 the population of Delhi had increased but not with Dilliwalas, the original residents of Delhi. It was populated by

---

125. This was the *kotwali* courtyard where the gallows were erected.

people who had come from outside. Gul-Andam's body had been buried in a trench near Salimgarh Fort. An old man was sitting there reading the magazine *Saqi*. He recalled that he had been present in the last assembly held by Gul-Andam. He had been a child employed there. He could visualize that scene once again. He was also present when Gul-Andam was hanged.

He wanted to call out to the prince and find out if some part of Gul-Andam still survived. Would the prince reply?

The thought had just struck him when he felt dizzy and fainted. He lay there unconscious for many hours.

28

When I Was a Prince

An old man had fainted near the Mughal Hotel in Bombay's Bhindi Bazar. Passers-by thought he must be some tired traveller who was still sleeping. Hundreds of homeless travellers would sleep on the pavements of Bhindi Bazar every night. However, when the old man didn't wake up at 10 a.m., the sentry on guard went to investigate.

The old man was very weak. He had a sparse white beard and his eyebrows were completely white as well. He had a wrinkled face and sunken eyes. He was dressed in a dirty patched kurta and a pyjama of some coarse cloth.

The sentry tried to wake him up but when his calls went unheeded, he came close and said, 'I think he is dead.'

Two passers-by bent over the old man and turned his face upward and found that he was still breathing but was unconscious for some reason.

The sentry called out to an ambulance and took the old man to the J.J. Hospital. The Parsi doctor examined him and said, 'Someone has poisoned him and the poison has spread. It is going to be difficult to cure him now.' However, he began to attend to the old man.

After a while the old man gained consciousness and said in a weak voice, 'Beti, where have you gone?'

His voice was so low that only the compounder could hear him. He replied, 'You are in a hospital. Your daughter isn't here.'

The old man replied in a very faint voice, 'I haven't eaten for many days. Please give me something to eat. My daughter has not come for many days. She used to bring me food. God knows where she has gone.'

The compounder gave news of the old man to the doctor who prescribed soup for him. The old man was fed slowly.

When he gained some strength, the police came to take his statement. A clerk from the police station had already come to check on him when he was unconscious.

The old man said, 'I have been living in Bombay for the past four months. I don't have a house and survive on the pavements. I have a daughter who works as a cook in a prostitute's house in Khetwari. She came to the pavement twice a day to give me a share from her food. However, she hasn't come for the past four days. I went to enquire at the house where she worked but the prostitute said that she had left work ten days ago and hadn't showed up since. I searched for her in many places but couldn't find any trace of her. When I had starved for three days and was too weak to walk, I lay down on the Bhindi Bazar pavement and lost consciousness.'

The police clerk asked, 'You used to beg, didn't you? Then why did you stay hungry? In Bombay city beggars earn more than graduates.'

When the old man heard these words, he became so angry that his eyes nearly popped out of their sockets. He said as loudly as he could in his weak state, 'That's enough, *Janab*! Don't utter any more nonsense. Perhaps you saw me begging with your father.'

The clerk was shocked by these words and gave the old man a tight slap. The old man fell down from the force of the slap but got up immediately and picked up the doctor's rule. He threw it with such strength that the clerk's head was badly cut and he fell down in a swoon. People rushed and caught the old man before he could hit the clerk again, as he seemed likely to.

The doctor took the clerk to the dressing room and attended to his wound. The police took the old man to the police station. A European inspector was present there. When he heard the details of the incident, he was very angered. Trying to retain his calm he said, 'Keep him in the lock-up till I hear the clerk's version.'

The soup seemed to have given a lot of strength to the old man who kept abusing the clerk.

After his dressing the clerk came to the police station and gave a complete report of the incident to the inspector. He got the old man out of the lock-up and once again started writing his statement.

The old man said, 'I will only give my statement when your clerk apologizes to me. How dare he call a respectable man like me a beggar?'

The clerk retorted, 'What respectability? You yourself told me that your daughter works in a prostitute's house. How can you claim to have any respect? If you are not a beggar then you must be a thug or dacoit.'

Anger once again pulsated in the old man's body. He was just about to hit the clerk again when the policemen caught him. The inspector threatened him, 'Stay where you are or it won't go well for you.'

'So did you bring a respectable man to be abused here? The blood of the emperor of Delhi runs in my veins. I will not tolerate being insulted and am ready to give up my life and take his.'

On hearing the name of the emperor of Delhi the inspector started laughing. He said, 'He seems a mad man to me. No wonder he is talking rubbish.'

After this the inspector started interrogating the old man.

'How old is your daughter?'

The old man replied, 'She is thirty years old. However, she is not my own daughter by birth; I adopted her. I had got her married but her husband died in the influenza epidemic. He was employed in Adam Bhai Peerbhoy's factory. When my daughter heard of his death, she came to see him from Bhopal and I accompanied her. We did not have the money to buy our return tickets. That is why we are in Bombay for the past four months. My daughter took up employment.'

'What work did you do in Bhopal?' asked the inspector.

'I used to work as a chowkidar in a rich man's house. My daughter worked there as one of the serving maids and I adopted her.'

The inspector continued, 'From which date did the blood of the emperor of Delhi start running in your veins? You said a while ago that you were his blood relative. How come a lowly chowkidar is making such tall claims?'

The old man smiled and replied, 'Since you all have come here, I have been reduced to becoming a chowkidar, otherwise before your arrival I was a prince.'

The old man's smile angered the inspector. 'If you were really a prince before we came, how were you reduced to becoming a chowkidar so fast? Don't babble like a lunatic in front of me. I have understood your worth. You are a very clever scoundrel,' he retorted.

The old man's face was once again suffused with colour when he heard these words. With great restraint he said, 'Yes indeed. You are acquainted with my worth and with yours! We destroyed and looted Ibrahim Lodi's dynasty thus we are sinners and you destroyed and looted ours, so you are one too.'

The inspector was furious but with great control over himself he asked, 'How much gold and silver did you possess that I looted from your house?'

The old man replied, 'All the gold and silver that Babur and Humayun looted from Ibrahim Lodi is now under your control.'

The inspector asked, '*You* are Babur's descendant?'

'Yes,' said the old man. 'I am Babur's descendant or rather was. Now, I am a chowkidar. In fact, now I am your prisoner.'

After this the inspector was silent and gave orders for the old man to be locked up in jail.

A Mughal Prince in Bombay

A Mughal prince lived in Bombay. He would dress in saffron robes and tie a sword at his waist. He was on friendly terms with the officers of the British government. The inspector called him and said, 'There is a man who claims to be from the royal family of Delhi. Can you identify him? Since you also claim to be a prince and are the son of Prince Dara Bakht, the son of Bahadur Shah, you may recognize him.'

That man came to the police lock up and looked at the old chowkidar. 'This is a false claim. He is no prince.'

The old man looked at the prince and called out, 'In fact, you yourself are not a prince.'

The inspector asked the prince, 'On what grounds do you say so categorically that the man in the lock up is not a prince from the royal house of Delhi?'

He said, 'I have no proof but I know each and every family member.'

The old man replied, 'I am older than you and know much more about my family members than you. Tell me, when Bahadur Shah went to Rangoon who were the family members who accompanied him?'

The prince from Bombay replied, 'Jawan Bakht and myself, along with Zeenat Mahal and Bahadur Shah. Bahadur Shah and Zeenat Mahal were in different tom-tom carriages. Jawan Bakht and I reached Calcutta in stages. There Wajid Ali Shah sent a tray of pearls as nazar but the British did not let him present it. From Calcutta, we went to Rangoon. After Bahadur Shah's demise I came to Bombay.'

The old man laughed from inside the lock up. 'The first lie is that Bahadur Shah and Zeenat Mahal were in a tom-tom. Everyone in Delhi knows that these two were in palanquins. Zeenat Mahal and Jawan Bakht were in one palanquin and [Nawab] Taj Mahal[126] in the other. The emperor was in the third palanquin and there was no one else with him.'

The Bombay prince looked flustered as he had concocted and spread a false story in Bombay about him being a prince from the royal family of Delhi. He was respected by everyone on that basis.

The imprisoned old man asked the Bombay prince many other questions but the latter could not answer any satisfactorily.

The inspector was standing by and listening to this conversation. He became convinced that the old man in the jail was being truthful, and thus, released him. He seated him in a chair in front of him and

---

126. Taj Mahal is a reference to Nawab Taj Mahal Begum, a wife of Bahadur Shah Zafar who accompanied him to Rangoon (Yangon).

asked him to relate the all the events that he encountered from the time of the *ghadar*.

The Old Man's Story

The old man said, 'I am the son of Mirza Khizr Sultan, who was the progeny of Bahadur Shah. He was shot dead after the *ghadar*. I was eighteen years old at that time. I was suffering from dysentery and was sick continuously for four months. I witnessed my father getting arrested from Humayun's tomb.

'In the evening when the news came that Mirza Mughal and Mirza Khizr Sultan had been shot dead, my mother left for Faridabad with me and my younger sister, as two of our servants had their houses there.

'When our bullock-cart reached Badarpur, we were surrounded by Major Hodson and Mirza Ilahi Baksh and their cavalrymen. The cart was searched and I was arrested. I was very weak as I was suffering from blood dysentery and my mother pleaded with tears in her eyes, "He is very sick. He has not committed any wrong and has been on the sickbed at home for four months."

Hodson sahib replied, "But his father ordered the murder of English women and children.[127] We will imprison him and investigate. If he is innocent, we will let him go. Otherwise, he will be executed."

My mother was very attached to me. When she saw that I was being arrested she ran towards me and caught me in a tight embrace. The officers separated her from me forcibly and made me sit behind one of the cavalry men and took me to the camp in Delhi.

I left my mother and sister weeping uncontrollably. She said, "My son, if your life is spared come and meet me. Go, Allah is your protector."

---

127. Reference to the massacre of British men, women and children on 16 May 1857 at the hands of the 'rebel' soldiers. There is, however, no proof that the emperor was involved in it. Zahir Dehlvi in *Dastan-e Ghadar* has written that the emperor, in fact, categorically ordered the soldiers not to harm the prisoners.

I was lodged with Samandar Khan, a Punjabi soldier, during my interrogation. He was a cruel tyrant. I had to keep going to the toilet because of my dysentery. When I returned, he would order me to clean the toilet with my hands. The first time when I refused, he slapped me hard several times. I was so weak that I fainted and ran a high fever all night. I continued my trips to the toilet in that state. I would suffer bouts of dizziness and stumble. But even in that state I would go outside to dispose of my excreta, every time.

I asked him for permission to go into the jungle so that I could be saved the bother of cleaning up after me. However, that tyrant refused saying, "You are probably planning to escape. You can't go to the jungle."

I was given very bad food to eat, because of which my dysentery was aggravated.

After four days I was presented before the senior British officer. The British informer, Gami Khan[128] gave witness against me. He said, "This boy used to accompany his father Mirza Khizr Sultan, to the ridge to fight against the British. When the English women and children were murdered in the Lal Qila, he was present there. In fact, he was the one who came out of the zenana mahal and said that the emperor had given orders for them to be killed."

On hearing this, the senior English officer ordered that I was to be hanged till death.

I said, "Ask him if he has seen me going to the ridge or coming out of the mahal himself or is he repeating hearsay?"

Gami Khan said, "I have seen it with my own eyes."

I asked him, "Where were you on the day that the Qiledar Douglas sahib was killed?"

---

128. Gami Khan, a criminal turned British informer, had been with the rebels earlier. Later, he joined the British as an informant and 'was responsible for the deaths of many people and for destroying various families' writes Khwaja Hasan Nizami in *Dilli ki Jan Kuni* (The Agony of Delhi)–one of his other books on 1857, included in *Majmua Khwaja Hasan Nizami* 1857 and translated by A Sattar Kapadia, and published online. He is mentioned as a British informant and someone actively involved in hunting down the survivors of 1857 by Zahir Dehlvi in *Dastan-e-Ghadar* translated by Rana Safvi (Penguin Random House, 2017).

Gami Khan fell on hearing this and bent his head. After a while he said, "I was in my house at that time."

I said, "You are lying. You were present there with the rebels and you yourself incited the rebels to kill Douglas sahib. I was present there at that time as my respected mother had sent me to Douglas sahib's guest, a doctor, for treatment of my dysentery. After the murder of Douglas sahib, memsahib and his guests you stole a silver vase and sahib's watch from there."

Gami Khan replied, "You are a liar. I was not present there at that time." However, he was so flustered that the English officer became suspicious and ordered that his house should be searched.

A search party was sent immediately and after a while the soldiers came back with the vase and watch. Apart from these, goods worth thousands were also found and brought from his house.

The English officer ordered that Gami Khan should be hanged.[129] He decided to release me.

I came to Faridabad but found that my mother and sister had not reached here. I searched for them everywhere but could not find them. I stayed there for some time till I recovered my health. After that I walked my way slowly to Bhopal since one of my father's friends, a nobleman, lived here.

When I reached Bhopal, I found that the nobleman had died. His family acted very carelessly towards me. Finally, I was employed as a chowkidar in another nobleman's house and spent my whole life there as his servant.'

After hearing his entire story, the inspector told the clerk, 'Undoubtedly, he is a respectable man. Apologize to him.'

After that he gave orders that a search should be conducted to find the old man's daughter. 'Till the daughter isn't found I will pay for his food and expenses,' the inspector added.

After four days it was found that some rogue had kidnapped the daughter and wanted to set her up for prostitution. The police found her and rescued her. The rogue was punished and the inspector paid

---

129. Gami Khan continued to be a British informer and was not hanged. Either the orders were rescinded or there is some error in recall here.

for the expenses of the prince and his adopted daughter to return to Bhopal.

The prince thanked the inspector profusely. He said, 'Don't feel bad but I was right when I said that Babur and Humayun were dacoits when they conquered Hindustan. But now, you all are dacoits. I was a prince then, and now, *you* are a prince.'

29

The Chef Prince

The Maharaja of Bhavnagar was staying in the Taj Mahal Hotel in Bombay. It was the month of monsoons and there were constant storms and rainfall. The travellers found it difficult to hear one another over its noise.

A seventy-eighty-year-old chef was employed at the Taj Mahal Hotel. He was considered to be extremely good at his work. The hotel would employ his services for their special and most important guests. His name was Qismat Beg. Since he had joined the hotel staff, he had shown many examples of his integrity and honesty. He had endeared himself to the hotel staff and his manager trusted him over all others.

One morning the Maharaja of Bhavnagar, who was lying in bed said to him, 'I have invited a few guests, inform the manager to arrange for a lunch for ten-twelve people.'

The soft voice of the Maharaja could not reach the chef's ears over the pounding of the waves and the constant noise of the rains. However, Qismat Beg's manners did not let anyone decipher that he was hard of hearing. Usually, he managed by reading the lips of the person speaking.

However, today he could not make out what the Maharaja had said. He came closer to the bed, and folding his hands asked with utmost respect, 'Whatever orders you have given will be followed but if it is not too much trouble can you please give me some more details?'

Since the Maharaja of Bhavnagar had not figured out that the chef had not heard him, he said, 'The ten people that I have invited are of the first rank and the arrangements for their lunch should also be first-class.'

Qismat Beg understood and replied, 'Your orders will be carried out to the last letter.'

With this, he backed out of the room with utmost respect, taking care not to show his back.

The Maharaja lay for a long time wondering about this old man who was so well-versed in oriental etiquette when others in this hotel followed Western manners. A desire to know more about the old man led him to press the bell and summon the room attendant. 'Today after lunch call Qismat Beg to the drawing room. I want to have a private conversation with him,' he ordered.

The attendant replied, 'Sir, he is a very ill-tempered man who behaves badly with the guests. I am afraid that he will misbehave with your highness too. He is very courteous when he is on duty and is very popular with the guests but is very unpleasant in his off-duty hours.'

The Maharaja asked, 'Why is that?'

'*Huzur*, he says that he is the emperor of Hindustan,' replied the attendant.

The maharaja was very surprised. He smiled and fell silent. After a while he told the attendant, 'It doesn't matter. You tell Qismat Beg that he should come for a private chat with me after lunch.'

The attendant saluted the maharaja and left the room as per Western etiquette.

After Lunch

After lunch, the maharaja, along with the editors of *Times of India*, *Bombay Chronicle*, *Sanjh Vartman* and some Hindu and Parsi dignitaries of Bombay who had come for lunch, came into the drawing room. The maharaja sent for Qismat Beg.

Qismat Beg came and with great respect presented three Hindustani salaams, salutation with an inclination of the body and head, and stood there with deference, hands folded in front of him.

The maharaja asked, 'Qismat Beg, who are you?'

Qismat Beg had deliberately stood near the maharaja's chair so that he could conceal his deafness and hear everything.

He replied, '*Huzur*, please forgive my impertinence but no one, including you, know who we really are and why we have been born in this world. We have been afflicted by the cycles of hunger, thirst, sleep, childhood, youth, old age, health and sickness.'

All the guests were astonished by these philosophical words coming from a chef.

The maharaja smiled and said, 'Undoubtedly none of us know the answer to these questions. But it seems you have tried to study the difficulties presented by life because you rattled off the names of all the cycles of life in one breath. Thus, I think you can answer my question.'

Qismat Beg responded, '*Huzur*, I am a man of Timurid-Mughal descent. By profession, I am a chef at the Taj Mahal Hotel. As far as age is concerned, I am old. By temperament, I sometimes feel child-like and sometimes youthful. Morally, I am an upright man. I do not lie. I do not steal. I refrain from cruelty and oppression. I consider it my duty to serve humanity. I may be a beggar, but I am the emperor of my heart. If there are any more questions, I will answer those too.'

His prompt, fluent and thought-provoking words forced the maharaja and his guests to give Qismat Beg their full attention. The maharaja asked spontaneously, 'Are you a Timurid *shahzada*, a prince?'

Qismat Beg had become very emotional by now. He said, 'I am not a *shahzada*, I am an *aahzada*, one afflicted by fate. I have borne all the blows of fate. The Timurid dynasty has now been wiped out. It had tried to subjugate everyone and make them their vassals; if not you, your ancestors must have once been its vassals. This question is now irrelevant and very painful for you and I don't want to get into its complexities. It pierces through my heart like a sword.'

On hearing these words, the maharaja bent his head and everyone else too lowered their gaze. After a while Qismat Beg said, 'Men should see their current circumstances only. Today because I am a chef, I have to follow your orders. I have understood that your highness wants to know the details of my life. I am not one of those who take pride in their past or regret it. Nor am I one of those who keep waiting passively for the future. *Huzur*, I am the owner of my past, present and future. This sky and land are both mine. This sea is also mine and all of you people sitting on chairs in front of me are also mine. And I know that this is also my reality that I am standing in front of you in a subservient manner. Nothing in this world belongs to anyone except me. In fact, I go so far as to say that no one exists except me. Only I exist, only I existed and only I will remain till the end. The sea is in its majestic form, frothing and spilling its waves on the shore. Soon monsoons will be over and winters will come and it will become a placid pond. I am the storm inside it as well as its calmness.'

The maharaja was amused at the philosophical and emotional utterances of Qismat Beg, but he controlled his smile and said, '*Shahzada sahib*, will you listen to me and take the trouble of sitting on this chair in front of me?'

Qismat Beg replied, 'Absolutely not! In a college the teacher keeps standing while the students remain seated. You are a student while I am a teacher; you are naïve while I am wise; you are all lacking in foresight while I am aware; you are all insignificant while I am significant; you all are important men while I am unimportant; you are all rich while I am poor; you are all mortal while I am immortal; you are bubbles while I am water; you are dust while I am air; you are the fuel while I am fire; you are darkness while I am light.' Saying these words, he started curling and twirling his moustaches with bravado. He started jumping up and down and repeating, 'I am I, you are not... I am I... I am I... whatever is, whatever was... whatever will be... there is nothing... there is nothing... I am I... I am I... hear it again, repeat it... I am I...- I am I.'

The maharaja and his guests were deeply affected by Qismat Beg's utterances and his frenzied movements. They were seized by a spiritual ecstasy.

After a while, Qismat Beg came near the maharaja and stood quietly. Then he said, 'Huzur, that conveyance has left. I was a markab[130] and my rider was someone else. I was a hotel and the guests were someone else. I was a bottle and the wine was someone else. Now you hear me, hear the story of this frail and helpless chef.'

Qismat Beg's Story

'I am the son of Emperor Bahadur Shah. My mother was his slave girl who attracted his displeasure later. I was ten years old when the ghadar started in 1857. In the agitation after the fall of Delhi, the emperor was not able to make proper arrangements for his wives, consorts and children. In any case, I don't think he would have thought of my mother for she didn't live in the Qila but outside it, in a house provided by the emperor in Khanum ka Bazar. He had appointed guards and sentries and even paid our expenses but he had become displeased with my mother before my birth and had never seen my face or called my mother to the Qila.

When all the residents of Delhi fled and Wilson sahib, the commander, entered from Kashmiri Darwaza, my mother left the house with me and set off on foot. The servants had already fled and there was no way to make arrangements for any kind of transport. My mother only took one hundred gold coins with her, leaving everything else behind. We headed for the Qadam Sharif dargah[131] which is a few furlongs away from the walled city of Delhi. Even though it is a short distance, the road seemed never ending since neither my mother nor I were used to walking. The residents of Delhi were running away from the city helter-skelter as if the day of Resurrection had come and it was each for him or herself, going towards God.

---

130. Anything upon which one rides
131. In present day Paharganj

Women with cloth bundles on their head were dragging crying and wailing children who were unable to walk. The men were in the same boat. There was no help from anyone and all were somehow trying to save themselves.

In Qadam Sharif, we found shelter in a dilapidated house. It was raining and I was very hungry but there was nothing to eat. My mother took me in her lap and tried to calm me down. The sound of gunshots coming from the city along with the screams and shouts of its citizens were scaring me and my mother both. I finally fell asleep.

In the morning, Indian soldiers of the British army came and arrested everyone, including my mother and I. They took us to the ridge which was quite a distance away. Our feet were bleeding by the time we reached. In the evening, we were presented before a British officer who questioned my mother. I don't know what the officer asked or what my mother replied. I just know that she said that she was the emperor's slave girl and I was his son. The officer gave orders for us to be treated well. Treating us well meant that we were given a small tent in which we spent all our time and we were given two meals a day.

When British administration was established in Delhi, we were sent to Chandni Mahal, a locality near Jama Masjid where other members of our family were also settled. A pension of ten rupees was fixed as a monthly stipend for my mother. Only I know the problems that we faced from my childhood till my youth.

There was a *khanqah*[132] near Chandni Mahal which I would visit often. I spent time listening to a dervish who lived there and his words had a profound influence on me. From him I gained knowledge about the truth of my existence and that of the universe and whatever I just said is the result of the time I spent with him.

My mother got me married to a girl in the extended family. I had children too but none of them lived. In Delhi, I became an apprentice to a chef and learned the art of cooking which is how I now earn a living. When my mother and wife both died, I shifted to Bombay and worked for different employers and hotels. I have

---

132. Khanqah-e Mazhariya

now been working at the Taj Mahal Hotel for many years. Since childhood I have been short of hearing, but since I am embarrassed by my deafness, I try to hide it.'

Upon hearing the chef's tale, the maharaja let out a long sigh. He asked, 'Who named you Qismat Beg?'

'My *qismat*, fate, gave me this name, for my mother had named me Timur Shah at birth. When I came to Bombay, I started using Qismat Beg as my name.'

The maharaja said, 'Come with me to Bhavnagar. I will give you double the salary you earn here. I just want to listen to you and would not make you work.'

Qismat Beg bent and presented three salaams saying, 'This is very kind of you and I am grateful, but anyone who has understood the secrets of this world is content to hold on to whatever they have and hold on to it tightly and not stumble around the world in search of more. I am given a lot of respect in this hotel and my temperament is understood by them. Even the sahibs who come here are tolerant of my eccentricities. I have everything I need here. You tell me why should I leave a place where I have nothing to worry about and go to your palace in compliance with your orders?'

The maharaja praised this attitude and wrote him a cheque of one thousand rupees saying, 'Use this for your expenses and you will get a cheque every year via the hotel manager.'

Qismat Beg took the cheque and started weeping. He backed out of the room and left.

God knows why he cried and which memory came to his mind?

Acknowledgements

I am grateful to Khwaja Hasan Nizami for documenting the stories of some of the victims and survivors of the Siege of Delhi in 1857 or they would lie forgotten in dusty graves in different corners of Delhi. Indeed, there must be many lying forgotten in dust in various parts of India.

There are many more stories that need to be told and heard of the victims and survivors of the Siege of Delhi in 1857: of their bravery and valour in fighting a colonial power and the sacrifices they made.

The translation of this book into English has been long overdue, and I am grateful and honoured to be the person to do it. I hope it helps in understanding the calamitous events post the fall of Delhi, into British hands, in 1857.

I have cried as I translated some of the stories and wondered at the transient nature of the world, after reading the stories of the Mughal princes and princesses and why we are so heedless of the future. I hope these stories act as a warning for the readers.

Sab thaath pada rah jaavega
Jab laad chalega banjara
All your grandeur will come to nought
When the nomad packs up and leaves

Nazeer Akbarabadi

I have been helped by many in this endeavour. I would like to thank Syed Shahid Mehdi who provided me with a copy of the book, *1857, Majmua Khwaja Hasan Nizami* which was published by Sang-e-Meel Publications in Lahore, 2007.

Saiyed Zaheer H. Jafri who has worked extensively on the events of 1857 has always provided unflagging support to my efforts and I am forever indebted to him.

Ruby Lal and Ira Mukhoty, who have always supported me and believed in my work. Their insightful blurbs add to the stories of these women.

As always, I remain indebted to my family for their love and support and especially my husband, Gazanfar, who has always adjusted his work and schedules to accommodate mine. Without a supportive and understanding husband it would have been impossible to work long undisturbed hours. I cherish the pride that my children Subuhi and Baqar take in my work and their constant support for every endeavour of mine.

I am extremely grateful to Jyoti Hasda for taking care of my home so I can work in peace.

And last but not the least, I would like to thank the team at Hachette India. It has been a privilege to work with Poulomi Chatterjee and Swarnima Narayan. And I am really thankful to Reya Ahmed for the gorgeous cover design that captures the true essence of the book.